Thomas De Witt Talmage

Sports that kill

Thomas De Witt Talmage

Sports that kill

ISBN/EAN: 9783741123177

Manufactured in Europe, USA, Canada, Australia, Japa

Cover: Foto ©Stingray / pixelio.de

Manufactured and distributed by brebook publishing software (www.brebook.com)

Thomas De Witt Talmage

Sports that kill

SPORTS THAT KILL.

BY

T. DE WITT TALMAGE,

AUTHOR OF

"CRUMBS SWEPT UP," "ABOMINATIONS OF MODERN SOCIETY," "FIRST SERIES OF SERMONS," "SECOND SERIES OF SERMONS," "OLD WELLS DUG OUT," "AROUND THE TEA-TABLE," ETC., ETC.

PHONOGRAPHICALLY REPORTED AND REVISED.

NEW YORK:
HARPER & BROTHERS, PUBLISHERS,
FRANKLIN SQUARE.
1875.

PREFACE.

TO save people from the Theatre as it now is, from bad books and newspapers, from strong drink, from ruinous extravagance, and from an impure life, as well as to suggest healthful forms of amusement, I first pronounced, and now print, these discourses. They have already been abundantly blessed and cursed by the people. I do not make in them the usual apology of haste, for they would probably have been no better if they had been carefully written out by myself rather than produced by reporter's pencil. I do not invoke the leniency of critics, but give them my full permission to stick in their quills wherever they may. That God will bless this book to the present and eternal safety of those who shall read it, is all I ask. The book is a sequel to "The Abominations of Modern Society," published three years ago.

I have not spoken with the tongue of a cynic. Life is to me a rapture. I know of no one who laughs louder or more than I do. But for the sports and recreations of life I should have been dead long ago. God has done every thing to please and amuse us. In poetic figure we sometimes speak of natural objects as being in pain, but it is a mere fancy. Poets say the clouds weep, but they never yet shed a tear; and that the winds sigh, but they never did have any trouble; and that the storm howls, but it never lost its temper. The world is a rose, and the universe a garland. When there are so many innocent things to please and recreate, let us keep off dangerous territory.

T. DE WITT TALMAGE.

BROOKLYN TABERNACLE,
January, 1875.

CONTENTS.

	PAGE
Samson's Sport...............................	7
The Bells of the Horses.......................	32
Fruit Speckled and Sour......................	51
Steering between the Rocks...................	75
Christian Gymnastics.........................	98
Theatrical Invasion of the Sabbath.............	119
The Wholesale Slaughter......................	142
The Crusade of Demons.......................	162
The American Plague-spot.....................	173
God-defying Extravagance of Modern Society......	197
The Shears of Delilah.........................	217

SPORTS THAT KILL.

SAMSON'S SPORT.

"And it came to pass, when their hearts were merry, that they said, Call for Samson, that he may make us sport. And they called for Samson out of the prison-house; and he made them sport."—*Judges* xvi., 25.

THERE were three thousand people assembled in the temple of Dagon. They had come to make sport of eyeless Samson. They were all ready for the entertainment. They began to clap and pound, impatient for the amusement to begin, and they cried, "Fetch him out! fetch him out!" Yonder I see the blind old giant coming, led by the hand of a child into the very midst of the temple. At his first appearance there goes up a shout of laughter and derision. The blind old giant pretends he is tired, and wants to rest himself against the pillars of the house; so he says to the lad who leads him, "Show me where the main pillars are." The lad does so. Then the strong man puts his right hand on one pillar and his left hand on another pillar, and, with the mightiest push that mortal ever made, throws himself forward until the whole house comes down in thunderous crash, grinding the audience like grapes in a wine-press. "And so it came to pass, when their hearts were merry, that they said, Call for Samson, that he may make us sport. And they called for Samson out of the prison-house; and *he made them sport.*"

In other words: There are sports that are destructive, and bring down disaster and death upon the heads of those who practice them. While they laugh and cheer, they die. The three thousand who perished that day in Gaza are as nothing compared with the tens of thousands who have been destroyed, body, mind, and soul, by the average American theatre.

The histrionic art arose in Greece. It was invented in the attempt to make great occasions of amusement and idolatry more entertaining and impressive. Although Sophocles, and Euripides, and other Greek writers dramatized in elegant and pure style, yet the chief theatrical spectacles of those days were scenes of the most disgusting impurities. As the nations plunged into excesses, theatres flourished, and dramatists were honored. The proud days of Grecian strength and courage suggested by Salamis and Marathon had gone, and the land that had produced a great army of orators, dramatists, artists, and architects, despised the restraints of Solon and Draco, and went into the shadow of death.

In the days of Roman prosperity, the theatre was prohibited, and not until the seven hundredth year of the great capital did this institution get a foothold. But once established, it ran a mighty career of cruelty and licentiousness, from the record of which common decency veils its face. The theatre of Marcus Æmilius Scaurus would hold eighty thousand people. At Nero's command, the theatres were covered with gold. Some of the buildings were so large that they inclosed trees and statues and fountains; and in order to cool and refresh the multitudes of people assembled in the play, a mixture of water, wine, and Sicilian saffron was prepared, and this was led through pipes to the highest seats, and from thence it distilled in fine rain that purified and cooled the air throughout the theatre.

The drama came on down through the ages, supported by the pens and the genius of some of the greatest writers and actors that the world has ever known. Dramatic exhibitions were first made in France, by the pilgrims who had come back from the Holy Land. Here were recited the scenes through which they had passed. Scriptural scenes were afterward enacted in a building in which were three scaffoldings, one above another. The highest scaffolding was arranged so as to represent Heaven, the middle the World, and the lowest to depict Hell. Although this was called a religious ceremony, the debauchery connected therewith caused Parliament to forbid it by a special enactment. But the drama arose in other garb, and won the sanction of the Government. In 1832 the French Chamber of Deputies voted one million three hundred thousand francs for the support of theatres, and to-day the most brilliant assemblages gathered in Paris are in theatres.

In England, the first exhibitions of this art were planned and conducted by the clergy, and were the Miracle Plays, or scenes in the life of the apostles, or the burning of the martyrs. The blasphemy of the thing arose to such a height that God was represented as acting on the stage; and, lest the play should be too serious, Satan and his imps were introduced to excite the mirthfulness of the audience. When England could no longer endure these outrages, "The Moralities" were enacted in a series of plays in which the virtues were allegorized. Faith, Hope, Charity, and Prudence came upon the boards. At one of these plays, enacted before the king, the actors became intoxicated, and Hope, Faith, Charity, and Peace staggered across the stage and fell, and were carried behind the scenes dead drunk. These plays were sanctioned by the king and by many of the clergy. A book containing an account of the various sports of the people was ordered to be read in the churches.

But the time in English history has come when the drama is to be extended to other shores. The manager of Goodman's Fields is to be sold out; but having displayed thorough honesty in all his dealings, his creditors allow him enough of a theatrical outfit to start again. With a troop of adventurers, he puts out for the wilds of America in 1752. The quarter-deck of the vessel was used as a stage for frequent rehearsals. After a six weeks' voyage, they landed at Yorktown, Virginia; and in Williamsburg, then the capital of Virginia, they hired an old store, and transformed it into the first American theatre. So wild was the surrounding region that, standing at the back-door of the building, the proprietor shot game flying past. Before the best people of that ancient town the dramatic entertainment was spread. One man with his harpsichord composed the orchestra; and, amidst rapt attention, the *Merchant of Venice* was played. From thence to Annapolis and New York these adventurers went. The whole country heard of their fame, and praised and condemned. In 1754, Philadelphia first saw the drama. The Quakers petitioned the authorities against its admission, but Governor Hamilton finally gave permission that twenty-four plays might be offered, provided nothing indecent or immoral should appear, and the manager should give security for the debts contracted by the company. On the first alley above Pine Street the first theatre of Philadelphia was opened to a great audience that rushed in, gathered by the novelties of the scene and the great excitement that had been raised. Since then, many theatres have arisen in honor of the drama; and the foot of every great actor in our day has trod the Philadelphia and New York stage.

At this hour the drama wields a mighty influence in this country; and although it comes down to us unexhausted by the march of many hundred years, and wearing garlands that many hands in all ages have entwined, we are not presumptuous when to-night we arraign it for trial, and, in the name of God, read the indictment, and demand of it, *Guilty*, or *not guilty*.

You say that the dramatic writings of the

world contain some of the best poetry, the finest sentiment, the most elevated morality, and Titanic strength of style, and the piling up by the giants of mountain on top of mountain, until on them they have scaled the heavens. I admit it. You say that the theatre has marshaled in its service some of the best poetry, music, eloquence, and painting. I admit it. You say that some of the purest of men have catered for the dramatic tastes of the world. I admit it. Witness Milton, and Dr. Young, and Hannah More, and Addison, and Walter Scott. You say that some of the dramatic writings of the world have had decidedly a religious tendency. I admit it. You say that some of the most astonishing talent that the world has ever seen has made its chief exhibition in the play-house. I admit it. Witness Conway, and Hackett, and Siddons, and Malibran, and Kean, and Foote, and Garrick. You say that theatres have done many noble charities. I know it. Witness the hospitals that have been founded, the destitute families that have received their benefits, and the wonderful charities that flowed from them just after the Chicago fire. You say that some people have gone frequently to the theatre without suffering any depreciation of morals. No doubt of it. You say that vast multitudes of people have, through the theatre, become acquainted with literature that otherwise they would never have had an opportunity of becoming acquainted with. I admit it. Witness the plays of Shakspeare, that are in the mouths of people who can neither read nor write. You ask, would not a theatre with virtuous actors, and an audience of perfect correctness in behavior, and where every thing was conducted in a Christian manner, be highly beneficial to a Christian community? No doubt of it. Such an institution would be an auxiliary to the Church. You say that you know theatres which answer exactly this description. Then I exclude such from any thing that I shall say to-night, for I come not for wholesale denunciation, but to do justice. A lie told against a theatre or a gambling-house is just as bad as any other lie. You say that some theatres are much more degraded than any thing I describe. Probably so. But I take all the theatres of this country, of whatever character, and strike the average. I have but one object in this sermon, and from that I shall not swerve. It is the discussion of the question, Should a Christian man favor the theatre as it now is? I say not.

First, because of its *deleterious effects upon the retainers and employés of the stage.* There have been connected with theatres high-minded and pure-hearted men, and I have no doubt that from this employment men have gone at last to heaven. But that the majority of the people employed in our theatres are of a most undesirable character will be, in general, admitted. How many of you would like to have your sons and daughters grow up and launch out in the association of play-actors? Would it be an agreeable prospect if you thought that your daughter would become one of the ballet-dancers who revolve so gracefully, and manage their feet in such a modest and unobtrusive manner? If a company of play actors and actresses proposed spending a month at Long Branch next summer, and should invite you to allow your son of fifteen and your daughter of seventeen years to spend that month with them, would you allow them to go? Nay; the disaster of putting your children five feet under the ground in Greenwood would be a hallelujah compared with it. W. B. Wood, the actor, in a book written in defense of the stage, speaking of his association with people of his profession, says: "How different is a theatre from our preconceived notions of one. A few weeks have shown me the vileness of envy and jealousy, and the pangs of disappointed hope and ambition. No one do I see of either sex even moderately contented. The greater proportion, particularly the comic department, are positively miserable." So much for the testimony of a man who knows all about it. Indeed, how could you expect a man who is, night after night, impersonating a miser, a highwayman, a libertine, a knave, or a murderer, to remain content, or pure, or honest? The man who so often assumes a bad character after a while becomes that which he represents. The associations of the greenroom are blasting. It is a terrific ordeal, through which but few can pass unsinged. The whole land ever and anon rings with some outcry of shame or cruelty that shows that many of the theatrical troupe are not strangers to the dram-shop and the brothel. The most prominent actors in the country have not suffered or lost their popularity by the discovery of their licentiousness. The crimes which wither other men seem to excite no astonishment when performed by these so-called "educators of public taste." Rousseau, who was never charged with any love for Puritanic notions or Christian sobriety, writes: "I observe in general that the situation of an actor is a state of licentiousness and bad morals; that the men are abandoned to low practices; that the women lead a scandalous life." Why is it, when you speak of a woman's attachment to the stage, you speak of it in a whisper, saying, "She is an actress?" Why do you not talk it out like you do every other occupation and profession? Show me one person connected with the theatre regularly, and for a long time, who goes about performing Christian offices, and serving God and serving his

Church; show me one such person, and I will show you a hundred who have been ruined for time and for eternity through the influence of the American theatre. Once holding a preaching service in Chestnut Street Theatre, before the service began, at the suggestion of Mr. George H. Stuart, we had a prayer-meeting in the "greenroom." It was a very strange thing to hold there. There are not many prayer-meetings in "greenrooms." Why is it that in England, and America, and Italy, and France, and Spain, and throughout the whole civilized world this profession excites suspicion? No unfounded prejudice could excite such universal disapprobation. Why does such a suspicion exist everywhere? Let parents, watchful of their children's associations, and sisters proud of their brothers, and men, intelligent, reputable, and Christian, answer.

Again, a Christian man should discountenance the theatre as it is, because of *its adjuncts of evil*. Find a theatre, and not many steps off you find the haunts of drunkenness and impurity. In the same building is a place where you may take a drink; and all around the place are solicitations to lust and wine. In almost every case, when a theatre is constructed, the property near it depreciates. The popularity and prosperity of the theatre can not be kept up in ordinary cases without these adjuncts of evil. Two of the largest theatres in London resolved to have no bar where intoxicating liquors could be purchased, and the abandoned were to be kept out as much as possible. The theatres went down, so that one was turned into a menagerie and the other into a juggler's entertainment. The managers of the old Tremont Theatre in Boston took out no license for the sale of intoxicating liquors, and passed a regulation that every female not accompanied by a gentleman should be prohibited entrance. The consequence was that the theatre went down—the manager in his report stating that the theatre would not have an audience under such regulations, even though the admission were free. Ay, the theatre would have died long ago but for the surrounding evils that keep adding fuel to these wasting fires of hell.

Again, a Christian man can not countenance

the theatre as it now is, because of *the character of the majority of the people who regularly attend it.* There are many persons every night at these entertainments who are of spotless virtue. Some of them go because they want to see for themselves. Some go as critics. Some go as ardent admirers· of tragedy. Some have an unbounded appreciation of the ludicrous, and they go to see the farce. Some, judging from the fact that they themselves have been uninjured, take their families. The splendid acting draws forth their applause, and they are unabashed by the indecencies that shine through the play or throw up their heels in the dance. But are the great audiences of the theatres made up chiefly of this sort? No, no. Husbands who have lost all love for home go there. Horse-jockeys go there. Thieves go there. The lecherous go there. Spendthrifts go there. Drunkards go there. Lost women go there.· The offscourings of society go there by scores and by hundreds. They block up the door-way. They hang over the gallery, and ogle, and smirk, and shout aloud in the applause that greets a brilliant passage, or one that caricatures religion, or sneers at virtue as prudery or overniceness, or hints at indecency, and makes the pure-hearted wife or mother turn away her head and say, "God forgive us for ever coming to such a place as this." An institution that nightly draws together from the lowest haunts of vice so many of the leprous, and unwashed, and abandoned, must have in it a moral taint. Walking forth in the fields, I see in the distance flocks of crows and buzzards hovering over a corner of the field. I can not see any thing beneath, but I know what is there—*a carcass*, else the crows and the buzzards would not be so multitudinous in that quarter. So when, in the community, I see the unclean and the reprobate in great multitudes swarming around an institution, I say, "There is a carcass there; there is death there." You are a merchant — you want a confidential clerk. You go to the theatre to get him. *Jack Sheppard* is being acted. You find a young man right before you, in a low theatre, entirely absorbed in the play. He evidently appreciates and approves. I think

I see you, merchant, leaning over and touching him on the shoulder, and saying, "Young man, I want a confidential clerk, and you are just the man I have been looking for." I do not deny that in every audience ever assembled in a theatre, there may be the good, the honorable, the pure, the useful, the humane, the conscientious, the true, the amiable. But are not the great mass of people that pour in and out of our theatres a different class. Woe to the man who sits, night after night, and week after week, in the hot, fetid, blasted, indecent companionship of the average American theatre! Good influences will retire from his soul. Gathering round him, with joined hands, will come ruin, debauchery, and wretchedness, to hail him into their brotherhood; and at last, having rent out his heart at a stroke, they will pour his blood into the cups of their carnival, shouting, "Drink! Here is to woe! and darkness! and death! and fire!" Dumas, the famous French novelist, who has written many plays for the theatre, says, in answer to one of his critics: "You would not take your daughter to see my play? You are right. But let me say, once for all, that you must not take your daughter to the theatre. It is not merely the work that is immoral—it is the play. Whenever we paint man, there must be a grossness that can not be placed before the eyes, and wherever the theatre is elevated and loyal, it can live only by using all the colors of truth. The theatre being the picture or the satire of social manners, it must ever be immoral, the passions and social manners being themselves immoral." Surely *that* man ought to know whether it is safe to take your families to the theatre! It is often said Abraham Lincoln died in the theatre, and the advocates of that institution think they have put a quietus on us when they have said that. But why do you not tell the whole story? He was shot by a play-actor. So if the theatre was graced by the presence of Abraham Lincoln, it was disgraced by the foulest murderer of the century.

Again, a Christian will discountenance the theatre, because it *has been the acknowledged avenue to destruction for great multitudes.* How often has a condemned man on the

STUPID BOARDING-HOUSES. 25

scaffold, in his dying speech, said: "*The theatre ruined me!*" The Bishop of Carlisle examined the records of a penitentiary, and found that the majority of the inmates were first seduced from rectitude by theatres and races. Alms-houses, insane asylums, and stateprisons have gathered the corrupt fruit of this corrupt tree. A young man comes from the country. He has heard a great deal about the theatre. He goes to what is called a first-class theatre for one night. The play is *The Merchant of Venice*. It does not startle him at all. But the next night, on the way home from the store, he sees a placard on the wall, announcing a different style of play, of most attractive cast, and the announcement that it is positively the last night. (When theatres are going to have a play for seven or ten nights in succession, they always put on the bills: "This is the last night.") The young man goes to his boarding-house. Every thing is dull. Something says, "You had better not go to the theatre; your father and your mother would not like it." But he must get into the open air. He starts along the street—his conscience bids him halt; but he goes up to the ticket-office of the theatre, pays the admission, and enters. At first he sits far back, with his hat on and his coat-collar up, fearful that somebody there may know him. Several nights pass on. He takes off his hat earlier, and puts his coat-collar down. The blush that first came into his cheek when any thing indecent was enacted on the stage comes no more to his cheek. Farewell, young man! You have probably started on the long road which ends in consummate destruction. The stars of hope will go out one by one, until you will be left in utter darkness. Hear you not the rush of the maelstrom, in whose outer circle your boat now dances, making merry with the whirling waters? But you are being drawn in, and the gentle motion will become terrific agitation. You cry for help. In vain! You pull at the oar to put back, but the struggle will not avail! You will be tossed, and dashed, and shipwrecked, and swallowed in the whirlpool that has already crushed in its wrath ten thousand hulks.

But I must leave until next Sabbath several important arguments against the average American theatre. Some of you will take no warning from what I say; but there are many here who will listen. The last time I spoke on this subject I said, "If there is a young man here who has in his pocket tickets to the theatre, he had better, before he goes out of the building, tear them up, lest they prove to him a ticket to perdition." At the close of the service a young man took from his pocket two theatrical tickets and tore them to pieces, and the sexton afterward picked them up, and told me of the circumstance. So may God send the truth home—not to one heart, but to a thousand hearts.

I stood one morning in an empty theatre in New York. I went in to satisfy my curiosity, and to look behind the scenes. Having examined the trap-doors and the side rooms, I came and stood alone upon the stage. While standing there, there came rolling up out of the silence into my fancy the scene which, the night before, might have been enacted. Pit, and boxes, and galleries seemed filled with a motley crowd. The stamp of a thousand feet announced the impatience of the audience. Suddenly the chandelier begins to blaze, and jets of fire leap along the ceiling, and the footlights kindle their splendor amidst the gorgeous scenery. A faint thrum of instruments arouses the orchestra, and lips to the brazen trumpet, bow to the viol, and fingers to the harp, and, with one magnificent burst of harmony, the audience are carried captive within the golden gates of sound. The play moves on. Princes stalk forth, and courtesans, not overmuch attired, come forth from palaces, and windows are hoisted from which gay ladies elope, and the heavy scenes are interspersed with the marvelous evolutions of the dancers, and pure sentiment and splendid oration are mingled with indecent allusion. In that seat is an artist, who has come to see the rendering of some famous passage, and through his eyeglass he watches every change of countenance in the actors. In this box are a father and mother, with their sons and daughters — the parents watching the play, the sons looking out on the galleries! Happy family! They have come to cultivate their taste, and to become better acquainted with human nature. Back yonder is a young man all caught up in the greatest enthusiasm. He laughs and cries, and chides himself that he has not before been to the theatre. He will not soon be absent again. He has started on the downward course, and what if he does go to ruin? It will be to the sound of the viol, and the step of the dance, and the enchantment of the drama. In that top gallery see them—the hard-visaged, the ill-behaved, the boisterous, the indecent. That poor soul was born in a mountain cottage. She helped her father watch the sheep on the hill. She used to bring up the cattle at night-fall, and well her foot knew the path to the spring in the rock. She wandered away. God pity that lost soul. No friend, no home, no hope. Fain would she breathe again, with light heart, the mountain air, and help her father tend the sheep, and go down and take a drink at the spring in the rock.

But the scene changes. Standing on that stage, the foot-lights seem to lower, and a mist arises before my eyes, until I can hardly hear or see the assembled audience. The theatre seems widening, and, at the same time, growing more dim. The pillars, from their dingy color, turn white, and the galleries look like a floating cloud, and the spectators that I saw grow into vaster multitudes — yea, ten thousand times ten thousand — and the air is stirred with many wings. The ceiling rises higher and higher, and changes as into a canopy of cloud, intershot with arrows of fire, and there is before me an amphitheatre, of height and depth, and length and breadth, and splendor and power such as I can not describe; and instead of the faces that were filled with mirth, and lightness, and gayety, I see an array of countenances filled with such earnestness as men exhibit who are on trial for their lives. In the midst of this great audience, which are like the leaves and stars for numbers, there begins to arise something that at first looks like a great cloud, then like a huge pillar; and afterward it grows brighter and flames out in glory; and, running my eye up and down the tremendous elevation, I find it is a *throne — a stupendous throne — a great white throne.* And there is an awful hush, and I see that the faces around are changing into deeper earnestness. Some kindle with highest rapture, and some grow pale with fear; and something says: "These are the generations of men assembled to give an account of all their deeds; and these are the parents who were faithful to their children; and these are they who corrupted their families; and these are they who plunged into earthly crimes and called them sports; and these are they who committed soul-suicide; and these are they who served their God, and found their greatest pleasure in loving him; and this—and *this is the throne—the great white throne*—THE THRONE OF JUDGMENT."

"And I saw the dead, small and great, standing before God, and the books were opened."

THE BELLS OF THE HORSES.

"In that day shall there be upon the bells of the horses, Holiness unto the Lord."—Zech. xiv., 20.

THE camels of Midia had bells which jingled as they went. The horses of kings and conquerors wore on their harness golden chains which made tinnabulation. My text prophesies the time when the music and the merry-making of the world shall be consecrated. In the good days that are to come, there shall be no less mirth and good cheer, but all shall be innocent. Now the clang of the bells often means dissipation and riot; but my text pictures the day when not only all inside the temple, but all outside of it, shall be under religious influence. "In that day shall there be upon the bells of the horses, Holiness unto the Lord." That this day has not yet come is evident from the present character of that popular amusement, the average American theatre, of which last Sabbath I spoke, and again speak.

I am asked about the influence of the theatre. The usual mode of discoursing upon this subject is to represent all play-actors as debauched, and the entire audience gathered in a theatre as abandoned and reprobate. Now what good can a man expect by such a positive misrepresentation? Nine-tenths of this audience have at some time in their life been in a theatre. You do not think yourselves abandoned and depraved. Do you not suppose that every night in some of our theatres there are men who go there for the same reason that took you? At this point, I wish to disclaim any sympathy with those who charge upon dramatic literature the crimes of the theatre. Any dialogue is a drama. Solomon's Song is a drama. The book of Job is a drama. Some of the parables of Christ are dramas. The piece in the old New England spelling-book, which represents a youth, Christ, and Satan in conversation, is a drama. You have no right to put upon the works of Shakspeare, Addison, and Walter Scott the fooleries and outrages of the clog-dancers of the theatre. Blot out from sacred and profane literature the drama, and you have destroyed whole constellations of beauty and purity. I love the drama, while I deplore many of the scenes into which it has been dragged. The drama is like the man who went down from Jerusalem to Jericho, and fell among thieves: it has been stripped and left half dead.

In my last discourse, I gave you five or six reasons why a Christian man ought not to favor the theatre. I said then that I did not speak of the best theatres or the worst theatres, but, placing them all beside each other, I struck the average. I add to-day that my objections to the theatre are confirmed by the united *evidence of the good and wise in all ages.* Greece and Rome, in the days of their strength, forbade it. The vast majority of the Christian people of Europe, and America, and of the whole world, have condemned it. The American Congress, in the time of the Revolution, condemned it. Josiah Quincy, in 1775, says, "The stage is the nursery of vice, and disseminates the seeds far and wide, with an amazing and baneful effect." Washington and Franklin, among statesmen; Socrates, Plato, and Seneca, among philosophers, have deplored its influence. Almost the entire testimony of the philosophic and religious world have been arrayed against it. But you say, "What do I care for Socrates and Plato?" Then I ask what is the evidence of your own Christian father and mother upon the subject? They could have had no motive in advising you against this institution, if it were not a good motive. You say that the theatre never had a chance to vindicate itself—so many people have been against it. I answer that it has had every possible opportunity to vindicate itself. It has had thrown around it all the fascinations of genius, all the arts of poetry, and painting, and eloquence. Notwithstanding all this opportunity of gaining the affections of the good, it stands up to-day for trial; and the noblest piety, and the purest philanthropy, and the best morality of the land sworn as jurors in the case, rise to render their verdict. Prisoner, look upon the jury. Jury, look upon the prisoner. Is it guilty or not guilty? "Guilty!" is the response, and so they say all.

Again, I discountenance the theatre because it *is the polluter of public taste.* The advocates of this amusement often recommend it as an educator of public taste. But look at the character of the plays. Is *Hamlet, Macbeth,* or *King Lear* a type of that which most frequently appears? No; stop on your way home to-day, and look at the placards upon the walls, and you will find a very different programme. If *Richard III.* were being enacted in one theatre, and the *Black Crook* in another, which would have the largest audience? While there are tragedies of unexceptionable caste, rendered with overwhelming power, a reference to the advertisements for nine-tenths of the theatres of this country will prove the depravity of the public taste upon this subject. You have not ink in your inkstand black enough to write down the names of scores of plays that are enacted night after night in the presence of approving gentlemen and ladies. By what law is an indecent thing any the less indecent by being on the stage? That which is improper before one person in the parlor, in a theatrical audience of fifteen hundred people is fifteen hundred times more improper. How would you like to have at a party in your house a score of men and women appareled as you have seen them, in the last three years, trooping forth on the American stage? Great scantiness of fig-leaves. One student of the play in modern days gives as a statistic that he counted seventy thousand immoralities. I do not doubt the statistician; but I think he was engaged in a sorry business. I should as soon think of going out upon the commons and devoting myself to taking census of the number of dead cats and dogs. Who can compute the number of the herd of vulgarisms, profanities, and indecencies that have, with filthy hoof, trampled across the stage? Educator of good taste! If there were nothing upon the boards of our theatres but good morals, and pure sentiment, and honest behavior, the upright might go there; but do you suppose that there would be such crowds of the reprobate in attendance on the average American theatre, or that there would come down such thunders of applause from the gallery? The elegant sentiment, the exquisite imagery raises up a few delicate hands, yet the applause is quite feeble. But the innuendo, the word that looks two ways, the emphasis that has in it a quaver of unchastity—how all the feet come down, and the hands clap, the sounds dying away only to come up with more boisterous and overwhelming outbreak. The pure men who go to such plays are disgusted. But they are in a small minority. If you should gather together in one audience all the theatre-goers in this country and in Europe, and put to vote in that great audience whether all the impure allusions of the play should be dropped out, a few hundred people would say "*Ay!*" But by hundreds of thousands of majority the audience will cry out, "*No! no!*" Educator of popular taste! Many of the refined, and elevated, and moral people have got along without its help. I think that there are enough innocent and ennobling amusements in this, as in all other cities, to culture good taste in the people, without the necessity of a resort to these very suspicious schools of refinement. Where the theatre has cultured one taste up to a higher standard, it has sunk a hundred lower. Educator of taste! A mighty missionary work is yet before it, for it must begin with the "greenroom," and work up through parquet and boxes to the top gallery; and this last will keep it busy in evangelical labors until the dawn of the millennium. Oh, benign and gracious institution! Show me one father or mother, brother or sister, son or daughter, that it has made a better man or a better woman. A few years ago the most popular play on the stage of New York was *The Drunkard*. It was said to be highly moral and reformatory in its influence. But what a commentary on the whole affair, that one of the chief actors of that play died in delirium tremens. The friends of the theatre make great boast of the actress, Charlotte Cushman, a woman pure and good, no doubt. I am told that when in her prime she appeared in the character of Meg Merrilies, her acting had no parallel. But I tell you the best thing Charlotte Cushman ever did on the American stage. It was last night, when, according to announcement, she forever walked off of it. *Exit:* Charlotte Cushman!

Again, the Christian man will discountenance the theatre, because it gives a *distorted view of life.* People defend it by saying that it gives one a knowledge of human nature. Put a young man in a dry-goods store, or in a lawyer's office, and he will learn more of human nature in six months than in a lifetime of theatre-going. Besides that, it is chiefly the worst side of human nature that the average play-house sets forth. Heroic Portia, and honest Gonzalo, and gentle Miranda are not types of the characters presented in most of the modern plays. What advantage is it for any one to sit down in an audience and look upon the impersonation of knavery, of libertinism, of unrelenting revenge, that looks out from behind the curtain upon sleeping innocence, and the knife that the murderer lifts, all dripping with the blood of the victim? If you want to see knavery, go look at it in prison chains. If you want to see uncleanness, go to the hospital, and look at the pile of agony and putrefaction. Do you want to see revenge?

Before you get through with life, some one will take after you, abusing you, slandering you, persecuting you, even unto death, and you will find out fully what revenge is. If men want to study these things, let them not go where they are surrounded by fascination of scenery, and palatial residence, and the crime is half excused by the skillful dramatist; but let them take a police officer and go down through the dens of the metropolis, and see at midnight vice, and loathsome bestiality and festering abomination, and breathe the sickening stench that comes up from the cellar where humanity wriggles in filth, and rots alive, and rends out its heart in torture, and blasphemes God, and dies. By the time you get through life, you will know more about human nature than you want to. There are multitudes of people who understand the world, its passions, its ambitions, its trickeries, its sources of power, its misfortunes, and who can touch the key of any emotion, and at will play the high notes of gladness, or the deep tones of woe, without ever having gone to this questionable school. But remember that hundreds of men are ruined by city exploration. They go to see for themselves. A man hears that lions are very dangerous. He says, "Is that so?" He opens the cage; and the monster with one stroke fells him, and with one craunch grinds up his skull. The lion never imagined that the man had come in to study natural history. Oh! the devil is mean. He says, "Come in and see." The man goes in to look for himself; the roaring lion grabs him, and he is gone. He learns *human* nature dearly who learns it at the risk of his *immortal* nature.

Again, I charge upon the average American theatre *much of the unhealth of this country*. The man who sits night after night, until ten or eleven o'clock, in the theatre, and then takes his oysters and his ale, and crawls into his bed at twelve or one o'clock, will be a sick man. No physical constitution can endure it. The nerves shattered, the imagination excited, the strength exhausted, he will be eaten up by disease, and pitch into an early grave. The American theatre has filled the land with an army of invalids. We see them dying with dyspepsia, with neuralgia, with liver complaints, and consumptions, and there is congratulation in hell that the theatre killed them. It is death to a man to be busy all day in a store, the air poisoned and corrupt, and then, as a usual thing, to spend three hours at night in a theatre, the atmosphere of which is made up of ten parts of cologne, fifty parts of tobacco, one part of oxygen, and three hundred and seventy parts of poor whisky. Oh! I have seen the average American theatre throw upon society a great many weak, inane, and corrupt men unfit either for living or dying. I knew a man in this city who was once foremost in the church, who came under the fascinations of the American theatre. He gave up the Sabbath. He gave up the Bible. He gave up God. He came to deny even his own existence, adopting the absurd theory that every thing is imaginary. He went many nights in succession to see *Macbeth* in the old Broadway Theatre. It blasted him body and soul.

Again, I charge upon the average theatre the fact that it is *the enemy of domestic life*. There are many places in this country where there are father and mother and children, but no home. The children are handed over to irresponsible employés, while father and mother are out at the theatre. Wherever it offers its fascinations children are a great nuisance. If the measles come to the little ones the week that Davenport plays, Davenport triumphs, and the measles go under. This institution has run its red-hot plowshare through hundreds of domestic circles. The average theatre is the sworn, bitter, everlasting foe of the home-circle. What will that mother say when she goes up to God, and God asks: "Where are your children?" She will say: "One of them turned out to be a defrauder, and another went off from home, and was never heard from again. I did all I could for them; that is, I gave three dollars a week to a good Irish nurse, and it was her business to take care of them."

And now I have some remarks of a more general nature. You must have noticed last Sabbath night, and this, that I have no sympathy with ecclesiastical strait-jackets, or with that wholesale denunciation of amusements to which many churches are pledged. A book just issued says that a Christian man has a right to some amusements; for instance, if he comes home at night weary from his work, and, feeling the need of recreation, puts on his slippers, and goes into his garret, and walks lively around the floor several times, there can be no harm in it. I believe the Church of God has made a tremendous mistake in trying to suppress the sportfulness of youth, and drive out from men their love of amusement. If God ever implanted any thing in us, He implanted this desire. But instead of providing for this demand of our nature, the Church of God has, for the main part, ignored it. As, in a riot, the mayor plants a battery at the end of the street, and has it fired off, so that every thing is cut down that happens to stand in the range, the good as well as the bad, so there are men in the Church who plant their batteries of condemnation, and fire away indiscriminately. Every thing is condemned. There are a great many who denounce ball-playing. They hate puzzles. They despise charades. They abhor tableaux. They say:

"Away with all parlor games!" They talk as if they would like to have our youth dressed in blue uniform, like the children of an orphan asylum, and march down the path of life to the tune of the Dead March in Saul. They hate a blue sash or a rose-bud in the hair, or tasseled gaiter, and think a man almost ready for Sing Sing who utters a conundrum. What do they prescribe for our young people in the way of recreation? *Prayer-meetings!* Now, a young man, busy in the store from seven in the morning until six at night, sometimes wants something besides prayer-meetings. We have a physical as well as a spiritual nature, that asks for recreation. Young Men's Christian Associations of the country are doing a glorious work. They have fine reading-rooms, and all the influences are of the best kind. I believe the time is coming when these associations will also supply physical recreations; when, added to their reading-rooms and to their prayer-meetings, there will be gymnasiums and bowling-alleys, where without any evil surroundings, our young men may get physical as well as spiritual improvement. We are dwindling away to a narrow-chested, weak-armed, feeble-voiced race, when God calls us to a work in which He wants physical as well as spiritual athletes. I would to God that the time might soon come when in all our colleges and theological seminaries, as at Princeton, a gymnasium shall be established. We spend seven years of hard study in preparation for the ministry, and come out with bronchitis, dyspepsia, and liver complaint, and then crawl up into the pulpit, and the people say, "Don't he look heavenly!" because he looks sickly. Let the Church of God direct, rather than attempt to suppress, the desire for amusement. The best men that the world ever knew have had their sports. William Wilberforce trundled hoop with his children. Martin Luther helped dress the Christmas-tree. Ministers have pitched quoits. Philanthropists have gone a-skating. Prime ministers have played ball.

This church to-day is filled with men and women who have in their souls unmeasured resources of sportfulness and frolic. Show me a man who never lights up with sportfulness, and has no sympathy with the recreations of others, and I will show you a man who is a stumbling-block in the way to the kingdom of God. Such men are caricatures of religion. They lead young people to think that a man is good in proportion as he groans and frowns, and looks sallow, and that the height of a man's Christian stature is in proportion to the length of his face. I would trade off five hundred such men for one bright-faced, radiant Christian on whose face are the words, "Rejoice! evermore." Between here and Fulton Ferry, every morning, by his cheerful face, he preaches fifty sermons. I will go farther, and say that I have no confidence in a man who makes a religion of his gloomy looks. That kind of a man always turns out badly. I would not want him for the treasurer of an orphan asylum. The orphans would suffer. Among forty people whom I received into the church at one communion, there was only one applicant of whose piety I was suspicious. He had the longest story to tell; had seen the most visions, and gave an experience so rapturous and profound that all the other applicants were discouraged. I was not surprised, in a year after, to learn that he had run off with the funds of the bank with which he was connected. Who is this black angel that you call *Religion*—wings black, feet black, feathers black? Our religion is a bright angel—feet bright, eyes bright, wings bright. Taking her place in the soul, she pulls a rope that reaches to the skies, and sets all the bells of heaven a-chiming. There are some persons who, when talking to a minister, always feel it politic to look lugubrious.

Go forth, oh people! to your lawful amusements. God means you to be happy. But when there are so many sources of innocent pleasure, why tamper with any thing that is dangerous and polluting? Why stop our ears to a heaven full of songsters, to listen to the hiss of a dragon? Why turn back from the mountain-side, all abloom with wild flowers, and adash with the nimble torrents, and with blistered feet attempt to climb the hot sides of fire-belching Cotopaxi?

The day comes when the men who have exerted evil influence upon their fellows will be brought to judgment. *Scene:* the Last Day. *Stage:* the Rocking Earth. *Enter:* Dukes, Lords, Kings, Beggars, Clowns. No sword. No tinsel. No crown. For foot-lights: the kindling flames of a world. For orchestra: the trumpets that wake the dead. For gallery: the clouds filled with angel spectators. For applause: the clapping floods of the sea. For curtain: the heavens rolled together as a scroll. For tragedy: the doom of the Destroyed. For farce: the effort to serve the world and God at the same time. For the last scene of the fifth act: the tramp of nations across the stage—some to the right, others to the left.

"These shall go away into everlasting punishment, but these into life eternal."

FRUIT SPECKLED AND SOUR.

"For a good tree bringeth not forth corrupt fruit; neither doth a corrupt tree bring forth good fruit. For every tree is known by his own fruit."—*Luke* vi., 43, 44.

CHRIST laid down this principle, and it is always applicable, and everywhere applicable. If you want to find whether an institution is good or bad, you have only to examine the kind of character it produces. I remember in my father's orchard there was a large apple-tree that yielded luxuriant fruit; but it had a hollow trunk, so that we boys could hide in it. Which was the best position from which to examine the fruit of that tree; in the trunk, where we sometimes used to hide, or standing on the outside, looking up at the fruit? "Well," you say, "standing on the outside looking at it." And so I really believe that those inside the American theatre to-day are less competent to judge of its immoral tendencies than those who are standing outside, and watching the products perpetually shaken down.

There laid two frigates off the coast alongside each other—the American theatre and the American Church. They were quiet for a long time. Although they had different flags, there had been no indications for some time that they belonged to hostile fleets. Indeed, there were small boats crossing over from one to the other so often that the people came to the conclusion that there had been a treaty formed between them, and that after a while the two frigates would come up side by side, bringing their different crews into the heavenly harbor. But three weeks ago to-day a shot went out of this port-hole, which has turned the opposing craft around, and opened a broadside of wrath, denunciation, and caricature which has filled the air with smoke and uproar. It seems as if all the cities had wheeled into line. Play-actors who never indited a stanza of poetry in all their life have undertaken to invoke the Muses, and there have been cards printed and letters written, and even the lightnings of heaven have been invoked for telegraphic assistance. Distinguished tragedians and comedians, after the curtain dropped, have come out in front to show that after all they are still alive! Chestnut Street and Old Bowery have been heard from. My secretary, who receives and opens all my letters (by-the-way, perhaps I might state now that I never get any disagreeable letters, for my secretary has instructions by the year always to destroy such, and only save those which are pleasant; I say that in order to economy on the part of those persons who like to save their letter-paper and postage-stamps), says, however, that there have been during the past two weeks a good many letters critical of the position that I have taken, some of those letters marvelous for bad spelling and a smell of whisky. One of them, I have been informed, told me to go to the company of the last being in all the universe that I ever want to be associated with. A distinguished play-actor met me, and with violent gesticulation continued to speak about the grandeur of the American theatre and its elevating tendency, until I was afraid he would tip over into my arms from intoxication, and if there is any thing on earth I do not want to fall on me, it is a drunken man, for he falls so indiscriminately. Notorious libertines and adulteresses have felt called upon, in the public press, to defend the grand and glorious and heavenly nature of the American theatre, and there has been an excitement for a great distance around, all because one plain minister, one Sabbath morning, attempted to answer the question of some of the young converts in his congregation as to whether they ought to patronize the American theatre as it now is. I am very thankful that I have been led, by the providence of God, to undertake this subject. From the amount of pus and corruption that has come out, I am sure it was time to thrust in the lancet. Sometimes I have shot at the devil, and missed him; but I am certain this time the shot has taken effect, from his roaring and howling.

I shall proceed this morning to answer some of the objections that have been made to the position I have assumed on the subject of the undesirableness of the American theatre as it now is.

First Objection.—" You have made a wholesale denunciation of all play-actors and all theatre-going people." I have to reply to that: The report of my first sermon on this subject unintentionally did me injustice. Perhaps the pressure in the columns of the papers forbade certain portions of it coming into print. Those who were not present at the delivery of that sermon, and the editors who criticised the position I took, will be surprised to hear for the first time that they have assailed me for a wholesale denunciation that I never enacted. I have in my hand the short-hand report of that sermon, taken by Mr. William Walton, than whom we have no more accurate or talented stenographer in the country. I shall read a paragraph from that report, to show you whether I indulged in a "wholesale denunciation," and I ask the gentlemen of the press who may be present to take what I read from that report:

[Mr. Talmage here read some portions of his first discourse, entitled "Samson's Sport," showing that he had admitted that good people had sometimes attended the theatre, and that there had been good actors and actresses.]

You say, "Why didn't you make this correction sooner?" I could afford to wait. I suppose the printing-press will go on for three or four years yet; besides that, I must confess to a very great fondness for mirth, a tendency I always have to be checking; and if there is any thing that gives me fun, it is to see people elaborately, profoundly, and learnedly answering something I never said. But while I admitted then, as I admit now, that there are pure people connected with the theatrical profession, and that there are pure people who sometimes go within the gates of the American theatre, I wish to reiterate that the influences of that institution are most baleful, and that if a man or a woman connected with it shall maintain his or her integrity for any length of years under these influences, it is because of most unusual and extraordinary force of moral character. At the close of my first sermon, an aged actor said, "Every word that that minister has declared this day is true; I know it from my own lifetime experience." In addition to the evidence of play-actors and managers who have testified as to the pernicious influences of the theatre upon its employés, I have this morning the evidence of Macready, a name mighty in theatrical circles, a name mighty all the world over. Macready, after retiring to Sherborne, England, in the evening of his days, wrote these words: "None of my children, with my consent, under any pretense, shall ever enter the theatre, nor shall they have any visiting connection with play actors or actresses." Macready ought to know.

Second Objection.—"You have no right to oppose the theatrical profession because there are bad men in it, any more than you have to oppose other professions and occupations which have bad people in them."

No doubt of it. Bad ministers. Bad doctors. Bad lawyers. Bad merchants. Bad carpenters. Bad shoe-makers. But are there enough bad carpenters to make carpentry disreputable? Are there enough bad doctors to make medicine disreputable? Are there enough bad merchants to make merchandise disreputable? Are there enough bad ministers to make the ministry disreputable? Oh, no! When your child dies, you will want a minister to come and read the service. But while all the other occupations and professions in life have not been overthrown by the fact that there are bad people in them, you know as well as I know there are enough bad actors and actresses to make the profession disreputable for the last two hundred years, and for the next ten thousand. I really believe there are in that profession more drunkards and debauchees than in any other profession that the world has ever known. I tell you the curse of God is on that "old mother of harlots." I prove it by the fact that when a woman goes through the temptations of theatrical life and maintains her integrity to the end, as did Charlotte Cushman, we gather around and build triumphal arches and spread a banquet, and celebrate it with poetry and song. Integrity under such circumstances was not at all to be expected, and the whole world throws up its hands in amazement.

Third Objection.—" Churches often employ at concerts and at fairs people connected with the theatrical profession, and therefore churches ought not in any wise to assault that profession."

I reply in the words of John Wesley, "The devil shall not have all the good music." I reply in my own words that when we find any music, any poetry, any eloquence, any beautiful fine art in the possession of death and darkness, we mean to capture it for God and for the truth. The devil has no right to music. He never made a sweet sound in all his life. He is the loafer of the universe! and anything we can take from him that he has in the way of fine art, we propose to capture. Nebuchadnezzar came up to Jerusalem, and he despoiled the Temple, and he took off the vessels of gold and silver that had been consecrated to God. He took them down to Babylon, and they drank out of them, and they drank until they were drunk; but while they were drinking there came a handwriting on the wall, and their knees knocked together, and their cheeks turned pale. Now I have to tell you that much of the music, and the eloquence, and the poetry, and the fine arts of the world have been dragged down into the Babylon of sin, but we mean to bring it back again to Jerusalem, and re-consecrate it to the Lord. And the reason that all theatredom has been turned upside down for the last two or three weeks is because they have seen the handwriting on the wall: "Weighed in the balances, and found wanting." Yes, my friends, we propose to take every thing that will be of any service in the Church of God. We want your cornets, your flutes, your bass-viols; we will take them all, and consecrate them to the service of Christ. We will come and take your best painters, and have them fresco our churches. We will come and take the amphitheatrical form of your buildings, and will adopt it as the best style of audience-room. After we have done that, we will come, and if your stilted and unnatural style of speech has left any eloquence in the theatre, we will take that, as when Spencer H. Cone stepped from the stage into the pulpit, and became an apostle in the Baptist Church, a star in the hand of the Lord Jesus.

I have been invited, through the public prints, to come to the Park Theatre and Old Bowery. I have been told I would be treated with a great deal of courtesy. I have no doubt I would. I now here publicly accept the invitation. I mean to come, not to see your plays, but to preach the Gospel of the Son of God, as it will be preached in every theatre on this continent. Under the auspices of the Young People's Association of Philadelphia, I proclaimed the Gospel one night in Chestnut Street Theatre. "All hail the power of Jesus' name" rang from the greenroom to the top gallery, and the Lord came down, and there were twenty souls that night that found the peace of the Gospel. And I give you fair warning, we are coming to take possession of your palaces. Surrender! Surrender!

We will not stop with taking the music and the buildings, for I now make public invitation to all actors and actresses, and all the employés of the theatre down to the clog-dancers and the call-boy on the stage, to come and give yourselves to God, and sit at our holy communion, and journey with us toward the good land which the Lord has provided for us. Come and wash in the fountain that cleanses our sins away. You can not afford to despise the Church. You were not brought up amidst theatrical associations. Some of you were rocked in the cradle of a Christian mother, and prayers enough have been offered for you to break you down into penitence, if you would only think. You had a Christian sister who died in the faith of the Gospel. You have a good many friends in the heavenly land waiting for you. You were made for something better than the life you are now living. You have received enough injustice at the hands of your theatrical employers to make you want to break away from the thralldom; and if you could get out from your surroundings, you would start this very day. I open the door for you. I invite you into Christian association. I commend to you the sympathy of the Lord Jesus Christ. By the memory of your better days, by the graves of your Christian kindred, by the mercy of an all-compassionate God, I beg you to come off that desert, parched and sirocco-struck, into the gardens of God! I confess it, we want your music, we want your buildings, we want your fine arts; above all, we want your immortal souls, for whom Jesus died!

Fourth Objection.—"The preacher, by his profession, is hindered from going to the theatre; therefore he can not know what its real character is."

Before I answer that objection, I want to say I have a right to go anywhere you have. When the Lord calls a man into the ministry, he does not put him on the limits. What is wrong for me is wrong for you. What is right for you is right for me. I confess that I have been but three times in my life in a theatre for the purpose of witnessing a play, and that in very early manhood; and yet is there no way of understanding an institution without constantly sitting in its presence, and under its influence? I have never seen the inside of a gambling-hell, and yet shall I forbear to tell the young men of my congregation of the danger of going to such places? I have never seen the inside of a house of shame, yet shall I forbear to tell the people of my congregation that those are the gates of hell? I have never felt the pang of physical disease in my body, not once; but shall I therefore do nothing for the alleviation of those who are wrung with physical torture? I will undertake to say this morning that I know as much about the theatre as any man in this house. I have seen young men by the scores go down under its influence. I have seen family after family broken up by it, the husband sent to his cups, the wife thrown broken-hearted into the grave, the daughter cast forth into a life of infamy. In this very last week I received a letter from a gentleman in this city in which he says, "Go on with your exposition of the American theatre. I know it is true. I had an uncle who had one of the finest of families. It consisted of a wife and three daughters. He got going to the theatre. He has become a confirmed inebriate. His wife sits in penury in a garret, and his daughters are waifs of the street."

There are people who sit this day before me trembling in the agitated memory of the fact that the theatre has sent its consuming fires through their own houses. Oh, it is a monster, so rampant, so cruel, so loathsome, so God-defying, I wonder the avalanche of the Lord's indignation does not slide down on it. Know it? I know it a great deal better than I wish I did know it. While there are exceptions, as I have said in former discourses, and am willing to admit now, I have to declare that, taking it all in all, the average American theatre is a sepulchre full of dead men's bones and all uncleanness, and wriggling with reptiles, and stenchful with putrefaction, and is the very vestibule of hell. "Oh," people say, "it has reformed. Why are you talking about the way it used to be?" My brother, I have been vigilant in the last two or three weeks, and I found out that there have been enacted on stages in Brooklyn and New York plays than which none more iniquitous, and dances than which none more obscene, were ever witnessed or heard of since the day when the manager of Goodman's Fields opened the first American theatre in Williamsburg, Virginia. Why is it that the *Black Crook* and the *White Fawn*, and plays of that kind, cease to shock the community as they used to? I will tell you. When those plays were first enacted, even the old theatre-goers sat aghast, and there was no applause for a while save by professionals, who had by managers been stationed around in the room to make demonstration. But people soon got used to it, and Christian men and women went to see the French nudities. They had a great rush for a time, and then they were no better off than other theatres. Why? *Because the other theatres got up something just as nasty.*

The theatres to-day are in full race. You want to know which will come out behind, and which will come out ahead? I will tell you. Will it be the Olympic, or the Park, or Conway's, or Booth's, or Wallack's, or Niblo's? I will tell you which one will come out behind. It will be the one that sticks the closest to what is called the "legitimate drama." I will tell you which one will come out ahead. It will be the one that panders most to the licentious and debauched taste of the great mass of the theatre-goers.

Another Objection.—"The evil is inexorable. You can't stop it, and you are only running your head against a wall when you try to rebuke it."

The same old story. I suppose that when Noah was preaching about the flood, after he had preached a hundred and nineteen years, people said, "You might as well stop. You have only got eight converts—that is about one to fifteen years. You will never get people to go into that old craft. You will never persuade them that there is a deluge coming." But Noah went right on, and he preached a hundred and twenty years, although he had in all that time only eight converts. I must say that I admire the spunk of the old man!

When Sodom was to be destroyed, two angels thought it worth their while to come from heaven to deliver from that city one man and woman; and shall I not preach on against this iniquity, and declare that there is a deluge of sinful amusement flooding the land, even though only eight people are saved? Shall I not go on, though I get out of the Sodom of theatrical life only one—only one? Besides that, I have received many letters from people who say, "We have been going there; we will never go there again." I have received letters from Christian fathers and mothers that have said, "We have set up a new rule in our house." And I believe that the discussion now started and taken up in different parts of the land will go on until it will save ten thousand young men from a life of dissipation on earth, and from a destroyed eternity. I believe Christian parents who have been lax on this subject will have other rules for their households; that in the last great day it will be found that God's truth was never wasted, and that though the people may still continue to rush to the theatres, their going will not be a contradiction of my theory, but only illustrations of the truth that, while wise men foresee the evil and hide themselves, the fools pass on and are punished.

Another Objection.—"Your notion is Puritanic and Methodistic." I thank you for the compliment. Although I am not descended in that line, I love the Puritanic Bible and the Puritanic Sabbath, and the Puritan's morals and the Puritan's God. The Puritan has left for this country an inheritance of righteousness which his maligners have never yet had piety enough to appreciate. Who would not be a descendant of John Carver or Miles Standish? The most consecrated vessel that ever came across the Atlantic was the *Mayflower;* and if our nation had always gone in the track of that ship, it would have escaped a great many moral and political disasters. "But," say some, "you are Methodistical in your ideas. That is the notion they used to talk about in the old Methodist meeting-houses." Oh, I thank you again. There is no grander collection of people in all the world than those to whom you compare me; and if my own denomination, which I love very much, should ever tire of me or thrust me out, I should go over, "horse, foot, and dragoon," to the Methodists. "But," say some with a sneer, though I can not understand exactly what they mean, "you are popular." That is sad enough. I never tried to win the favor of the public by preaching a namby-pamby, sentimental, gushing Gospel. My religion is not a jelly-fish, but a vertebrate. It has backbone, and tells of God's justice as well as God's mercy; and I have not in anywise, as you know, made a compromise of public iniquities. If, notwithstanding all that, I have this sin upon me of being popular, it is not my fault. I have been running with my theology for fifteen years in the teeth of the wind, and if people will not hate me I can not help it.

But once more: The objection is made, "Your position on the subject is dangerous. Don't you know there is a vast amount of money involved in this thing?" Yes. "Don't you know that one actress went off from this country some years ago, carrying with her sixty thousand dollars, made by fifteen weeks of indelicate acting on the stage?" Yes, I know it. You say, "Don't you know that many of the printing-presses of the land get a great deal of advertising patronage from the theatre, and they may oppose you?" I suppose they may.

I have been told by my secretary, as well as told by some of my friends, that there have been in this case threats of personal violence unless I would desist. Why, people of Brooklyn, if all the world oppose me, I shall go right on, for I know I am right. This battle is God's, not mine. As to those who wrote the anonymous letters threatening me with personal violence, let the cowards step forth! You have said you would break my head. It is all uncovered, and this is a good time to break it. Several have threatened the use of the assassin's dagger and of fire-arms; and was there ever an easier mark than myself standing just here, with no pulpit even on the platform to hide behind? Take aim and fire! I shall go unattended every day and every night to my home by way of Lafayette Avenue, and not one of you will dare put the weight of your little finger on me. "The Lord of Hosts is with us, the God of Jacob is our refuge."

My position on this subject is confirmed by the evidence which has been given by nine-tenths of the decent printing-presses of this country. While they have differed with me in a great many respects, and sometimes violently differed, I will undertake to say that nine-tenths of the newspapers of this cluster of cities have admitted that there are gigantic wrongs and outrages connected with the American theatre as it now is. They say the way to do is to reform it. I say it never can be reformed. The Lord Almighty, by the brightness of his coming, will in his good time destroy it. It has had every possible advantage of vindicating itself. It has had all art and poetry and music, and yet it stands up in the cities of Brooklyn and New York to-day a monster of iniquity.

The *Quarterly Christian Spectator* gives this recipe for making a drama: "Sixteen pounds of powdered brimstone for lightning, twenty-four peals of thunder, a dozen bloody daggers, a skull and cross-bones, forty battle-axes, six terrific combats, three of them double-handed, a course of violations, eight murders, a pair of ensanguined shirts, one comic song, three hundred oaths, and sixty-four pages of blasphemy." Oh, it is depraved beyond reformation. A committee of the English Parliament went out to examine it, and came back and reported to Parliament that the only way to reform the theatre was to burn it down.

Now that is a poor prescription. By the triumph of God's grace, and great revivals of religion, let the theatres be turned into churches, their men of genius become preachers of the Gospel, their singers belong to the choir, the greenroom become the vestry, and the trapdoor be the place where you shall throw down all the unclean manuscript plays of the last half century.

But I must pause at this point. I shall not leave this subject incomplete, for I shall go on next Sabbath morning, and the following Sabbath morning, and show what is the principle to guide us in all amusements. I shall show the fearful invasion that they are now attempting to make in New York and Brooklyn, by introducing secular amusements on God's holy day, an outrage which, if the whole Christian world does not rouse up against, will overwhelm us with iniquity. I must go on until the charge shall not be made against me as it has been against many of the ministers of the Gospel, "You tell us what we can't do, but don't tell us something we may do." I shall go on and show what are lawful Christian amusements, and what are the principles to guide us.

But our hour for adjourning has already come, and the last hour of our life will soon be here, and from that hour we will review this day's proceedings. It will be a solemn hour. If from our death-pillow we have to look back and see a life spent in sinful amusement, there will be a dart that will strike through our soul sharper than the dagger with which Virginius slew his child. The memory of the past will make us quake like Macbeth. The iniquities and rioting through which we have passed will come upon us, weird and skeleton as Meg Merrilies. Death, the old Shylock, will demand, and take, the remaining pound of flesh and the remaining drop of blood; and upon our last opportunity for repentance, and our last chance for heaven, the curtain will forever drop.

STEERING BETWEEN THE ROCKS.

"They shall teach my people the difference between the holy and profane, and cause them to discern between the unclean and the clean."—*Ezek.* xliv., 23.

IN pursuance of that authority, I come to-day, to draw the line between right and wrong amusements. Indeed, it is a line drawn by the hand of God, and reaching from eternity to eternity. On one side of the line it is all right, and on the other side of the line it is all wrong. I have for three or four Sabbaths been arguing against that monster of iniquity, the average American theatre as it was and is. The nine arguments I have brought against it have in nowise been answered, save by scurrility and vulgarism and low abuse, which, instead of overthrowing the position I have taken, only strongly illustrate the depraving influence of the American theatre upon its retainers and employés. This morning I pass on to lay down certain principles by which you may judge in regard to any amusement or recreation, finding out for yourself whether it is right, or whether it is wrong.

I remark, in the first place, that you can judge of the moral character of any amusement by its *healthful result, or by its baleful reaction.* There are people who seem made up of hard facts. They are a combination of multiplication tables and statistics. If you show them an exquisite picture, they will begin to discuss the pigments involved in the coloring. If you show them a beautiful rose, they will submit it to a botanical analysis, which is only the *post-mortem* examination of a flower. They have no rebound in their nature. They never do any thing more than smile. There are no great tides of feeling surging up from the depths of their soul, in billow after billow of reverberating laughter. They seem as if nature had built them by contract, and made a bungling job out of it. But blessed be God, there are people in the world who have bright faces, and whose life is a song, an anthem, a pæan of victory.

Even their troubles are like the vines that crawl up the side of a great tower, on the top of which the sunlight sits, and the soft airs of summer hold perpetual carnival. They are the people you like to have come to your house; they are people I like to have come to my house. If you but touch the hem of their garments, you are healed.

Now it is these exhilarant and sympathetic and warm-hearted people that are most tempted to pernicious amusements. In proportion as a ship is swift, it wants a strong helmsman; in proportion as a horse is gay, it wants a stout driver; and these people of exuberant nature will do well to look at the reaction of all their amusements. If an amusement sends you home at night nervous so that you can not sleep, and you rise up in the morning, not because you are slept out, but because your duty drags you from your slumbers, you have been where you ought not to have been. There are amusements that send a man next day to his work bloodshot, yawning, stupid, nauseated; and they are wrong kinds of amusement. There are entertainments that give a man disgust with the drudgery of life, with tools because they are not swords, with working aprons because they are not robes, with cattle because they are not infuriated bulls of the arena. If any amusement sends you home longing for a life of romance and thrilling adventure, love that takes poison and 'shoots itself, moonlight adventures and hair-breadth escapes, you may depend upon it that you are the sacrificed victim of unsanctified pleasure. Our recreations are intended to build us up; and if they pull us down as to our moral or as to our physical strength, you may come to the conclusion that they are in the class spoken of by my text as obnoxious.

Still further: Those amusements are wrong which *lead you into expenditure beyond your means.* Money spent in recreation is not thrown away. It is all folly for us to come from a place of amusement feeling that we have wasted our money and time. You may by it have made an investment worth more than the transaction that yielded you a hundred or a thousand dollars. But how many properties have been riddled by costly amusements?

The table has been robbed to pay the club. The Champagne has cheated the children's wardrobe. The carousing-party has burned up the boy's primer. The table-cloth of the corner saloon is in debt to the wife's faded dress. Excursions that in a day make a tour around a whole month's wages; ladies whose lifetime business it is to "go shopping;" bets on horses, and a box at the theatre have their counterparts in uneducated children, bankruptcies that shock the money market and appall the Church, and that send drunkenness staggering across the richly-figured carpet of the mansion, and dashing into the mirror, and drowning out the carol of music with the whooping of bloated sons come home to break their old mother's heart.

I saw a beautiful home, where the bell rang violently late at night. The son had been off in sinful indulgences. His comrades were bringing him home. They carried him to the door. They rang the bell at one o'clock in the morning. Father and mother came down. They were waiting for the wandering son, and then the comrades, as soon as the door was opened, threw the prodigal headlong into the door-way, crying, "There he is, drunk as a fool. Ha, ha!" When men go into amusements that they can not afford, they first borrow what they can not earn, and then they steal what they can not borrow. First they go into embarrassment, and then into lying, and then into theft; and when a man gets as far on as that, he does not stop short of the penitentiary. There is not a prison in the land where there are not victims of unsanctified amusements.

How often I have had parents come to me and ask me to go over to New York and beg their boy off from crimes that he had committed against his employer—the taking of funds out of the employer's till, or the disarrangement of the accounts. Why, he had salary enough to pay all lawful expenditure, but not enough salary to meet his sinful amusements. And again and again I have gone and implored for the young man, sometimes, alas! the petition all unavailing. Merchant of New York, is there a disarrangement in your accounts? Is there a leakage in your money-drawer? Did not the cash account come out right last night? I will tell you. There is a young man in your store wandering off into bad amusements. The salary you give him may meet lawful expenditures, but not the sinful indulgences in which he has entered, and he takes by theft that which you do not give him in lawful salary.

How brightly the path of unrestrained amusement opens. The young man says, "Now I am off for a good time. Never mind economy. I'll get money somehow. What splendid acting in this theatre to-night! What a fine road! What a beautiful day for a ride! Crack the whip, and over the turnpike! Come, boys, fill high your glasses. Drink! Long life, health, plenty of rides just like this!" Hard-working men hear the clatter of the hoofs, and look up and say, "Why, I wonder where those fellows get their money from. We have to toil and drudge. They do nothing." To these gay men life is a thrill and an excitement. They stare at other people, and in turn are stared at. The watch-chain jingles. The cup foams. The cheeks flush. The eyes flash. The midnight hears

4*

their guffaw. They swagger. They jostle decent men off the sidewalk. They take the name of God in vain. They parody the hymn they learned at their mother's knee; and to all pictures of coming disaster they cry out, "Who cares!" and to the counsel of some Christian friend, "Who are you!" Passing along the street some night, you hear a shriek in a grog-shop, the rattle of the watchman's club, the rush of the police. What is the matter now? Oh, this reckless young man has been killed in a grog-shop fight. Carry him home to his father's house. Parents will come down and wash his wounds, and close his eyes in death. They forgive him all he ever did, though he can not in his silence ask it. The prodigal has got home at last. Mother will go to her little garden, and get the sweetest flowers, and twist them into a chaplet for the silent heart of the wayward boy, and push back from the bloated brow the long locks that were once her pride. And the air will be rent with the father's cry, "Oh, my son, my son, my poor son! Would God I had died for thee, oh, my son, my son!"

I go further, and say those are unchristian amusements which become *the chief business of a man's life.* Life is an earnest thing. Whether we were born in a palace or a hovel; whether we are affluent, or pinched, we have to work. If you do not sweat with toil, you will sweat with disease. You have a soul that is to be transfigured amidst the pomp of a judgment-day; and after the sea has sung its last chant, and the mountain shall have come down in an avalanche of rock, you will live and think and act, high on a throne where seraphs sing, or deep in a dungeon where demons howl. In a world where there is so much to do for yourselves, and so much to do for others, God pity that man who has nothing to do.

Your sports are merely means to an end. They are alleviations and helps. The arm of toil is the only arm strong enough to bring up the bucket out of the deep well of pleasure. Amusement is only the bower where business and philanthropy rest while on their way to stirring achievements. Amusements are merely the vines that grow about the anvil of toil, and the blossoming of the hammers.

Alas for the man who spends his life in laboriously doing nothing, his days in hunting up lounging-places and loungers, his nights in seeking out some gas-lighted foolery! The man who always has on his sporting-jacket, ready to hunt for game in the mountain or fish in the brook, with no time to pray, or work, or read, is not so well off as the greyhound that runs by his side, or the fly-bait with which he whips the stream.

A man who does not work does not know how to play. If God had intended us to do nothing but laugh, we would have been all mouth; but he has given us shoulders with which to lift, and hands with which to work, and brains with which to think. The amusements of life are merely the orchestra playing while the great tragedy of life plunges through its five acts—infancy, childhood, manhood, old age, and death. Then *exit* the last chance for mercy. *Enter* the overwhelming realities of an eternal world!

I go further, and say that all those amusements are wrong *which lead into bad company*. If you belong to an organization where you have to associate with the intemperate, with the unclean, with the abandoned, however well they may be dressed, in the name of God quit it. They will despoil your nature. They will undermine your moral character. They will drop you when you are destroyed. They will give not one cent to support your children when you are dead. They will weep not one tear at your burial. They will chuckle over your damnation.

I had a friend at the West—a rare friend. He was one of the first to welcome me to my new home. To fine personal appearance, he added a generosity, frankness, and ardor of nature that made me love him like a brother. But I saw evil people gathering around him. They came up from the saloons, from the theatres, from the gambling-hells. They plied him with a thousand arts. They seized upon his social nature, and he could not stand the charm. They drove him on the rocks, like a ship full-winged, shivering on the breakers. I used to admonish him. I would say, "Now I wish you would quit these bad habits, and become a Christian." "Oh," he would reply,

"I would like to; I would like to; but I have gone so far I don't think there is any way back." In his moments of repentance, he would go home and take his little girl of eight years, and embrace her convulsively, and cover her with adornments, and strew around her pictures and toys, and every thing that could make her happy; and then, as though hounded by an evil spirit, he would go out to the inflaming cup and the house of shame, like a fool to the correction of stocks.

I was summoned to his death-bed. I hastened. I entered the room. I found him, to my surprise, lying in full every-day dress on the top of the couch. I put out my hand. He grasped it excitedly, and said, "Sit down, Mr. Talmage, right there." I sat down. He said, "Last night I saw my mother, who has been dead twenty years, and she sat just where you sit now. It was no dream. I was wide awake. There was no delusion in the matter. I saw her just as plainly as I see you.—"Wife, I wish you would take these strings off of me. There are strings spun all around my body. I wish you would take them off of me." I saw it was delirium. "Oh," replied his wife, "my dear, there is nothing there, there is nothing there." He went on, and said, "Just where you sit, Mr. Talmage, my mother sat. She said to me, 'Roswell, I do wish you would do better.' I got out of bed, put my arms around her, and said, 'Mother, I want to do better. I have been trying to do better. Won't you help me to do better? You used to help me.' No mistake about it, no delusion. I saw her — the cap and the apron and the spectacles, just as she used to look twenty years ago. But I do wish you would take these strings away. They annoy me so. I can hardly talk. Won't you take them away?" I knelt down and prayed, conscious of the fact that he did not realize what I was saying. I got up. I said, "Good-bye; I hope you will be better soon." He said, "Good-bye, good-bye."

That night his soul went to the God who gave it. Arrangements were made for the obsequies. Some said, "Don't bring him in the church; he was too dissolute." "Oh," I said, "bring him. He was a good friend of mine while he was alive, and I shall stand by him now that he is dead. Bring him to the church."

As I sat in the pulpit and saw his body coming up through the aisle, I felt as if I could weep tears of blood. I told the people that day, "This man had his virtues, and a good many of them. He had his faults, and a good many of them. But if there is any man in this audience who is without sin, let him cast the first stone at this coffin-lid." On one side the pulpit sat that little child, rosy, sweet-faced, as beautiful as any little child that sat at your table this morning, I warrant you. She looked up wistfully, not knowing the full sorrows of an orphan child. Oh, her countenance haunts me to-day, like some sweet face looking upon us through a horrid dream. On the other side of the pulpit were the men who had destroyed him. There they sat, hard-visaged, some of them pale from exhausting disease, some of them flushed until it seemed as if the fires of iniquity flamed through the cheek and crackled the lips. They were the men who had done the work. They were the men who had bound him hand and foot. They had kindled the fires. They had poured the wormwood and gall into that orphan's cup. Did they weep? No. Did they sigh repentingly? No. Did they say, "What a pity that such a brave man should be slain?" No, no; not one bloated hand was lifted to wipe a tear from a bloated cheek. They sat and looked at the coffin like vultures gazing at the carcass of a lamb whose heart they had ripped out! I cried in their ears as plainly as I could, "There is a God and a judgment-day, and an awful hell for those who destroy their fellows." Did they tremble? Oh no, no. They went back from the house of God, and that night, though their victim laid in Oakwood Cemetery, I was told that they blasphemed, and they drank, and they gambled, and there was not one less customer in all the houses of iniquity. This destroyed man was a Samson in physical strength, but Delilah sheared him, and the Philistines of evil companionship dug his eyes out and threw him into the prison of evil habits, and "he made sport for them." But in the hour of his death he rose up and took hold of the two pillared curses of God against drunkenness and uncleanness, and threw himself forward, until down upon him and his companions there came the thunders of an eternal catastrophe. Oh, beware of evil companionship. "Rejoice, O young man, in thy youth; and let thy heart cheer thee in the days of thy youth, and walk in the ways of thine heart, and in the sight of thine eyes: but know thou, that for all these things God will bring thee into judgment."

I want to offer one more rule. Any amusement that gives you a distaste for domestic life is bad. How many bright domestic circles have been broken up by sinful amusements! The father went off, the mother went off, the child went off. There are to-day the fragments before me of a great many blasted households. Oh, if you have wandered away, I would like to charm you back by the sound of that one word "home." Do you not know that you have but little more time to give to domestic welfare? Do you not see, father, that your children are soon to go out into the world, and all the influence for good you are to have over them you must have now? Death will break in on your conjugal relations, and alas, if you have to stand over the grave of one who perished from your neglect!

I saw a wayward husband standing at the death-bed of his Christian wife, and I saw her point to a ring on her finger, and heard her say to her husband, "Do you see that ring?" He replied, "Yes, I see it." "Well," said she, "do you remember who put it there?" "Yes," said he, "I put it there;" and all the past seemed to rush upon him. By the memory of that day when, in the presence of men and angels, you promised to be faithful in joy and sorrow, and in sickness and in health; by the memory of those pleasant hours when you sat together in your new home talking of a bright future; by the cradle and the joyful hour when one life was spared and another given; by that sick-bed, when the little one lifted up the hands and called for help, and you knew he must die, and he put one arm around each of your necks and brought you very near together in that dying kiss; by the little grave in Greenwood that you never think of without a rush of tears; by the family Bible, where, amidst stories of heavenly love, is the brief but expressive record of births and deaths; by the neglects of the past, and by the agonies of the future; by a judgment-day, when husbands and wives, parents and children, in immortal groups, will stand to be caught up in shining array, or to shrink down into darkness; by all that, I beg you give to home your best affections. I look in your eyes to-day, and I ask you the question that Gehazi asked of the Shunamite: "Is it well with thee? Is it well with thy husband? Is it well with thy child?" God grant that it may be everlastingly well.

By these four or five rules I want you to try all amusements, and I especially want you to try the American theatre — an institution of which I have been speaking for two or three Sabbaths. It can not stand the test. It is a war on home, it is a war on physical health, it is a war on man's moral nature. This is the broad avenue through which tens of thousands press into the grog-shop and the brothel. Oh, Christian people, stand back from it. Do not say, "I go sometimes;" stand back from it.

The Rev. Dr. Hatfield, of New York, once said to me, "I used to go to the theatre when I was a young man. While I was in town, a Christian friend from the country came to the city. She was visiting at a friend's house. I went down to see her, and found that she had gone to the theatre. I went to the theatre. I got inside, and I looked, and there I saw her fascinated with an objectionable play, and I said, 'Is it possible, this Christian woman looking at such things as these!' although I was not a Christian man, I said, 'I'll never come to the theatre again;' and that was the last time I was ever there. The incongruity of a Christian at the theatre drove me back from all such indulgences." They tell me that sometimes ministers of the Gospel go to such places. There may be some here, or there may be some to whom these words shall come, who thus stultify themselves, and make themselves obnoxious to God. Let me tell you of a minister of the Gospel who went to a theatre in Boston some years ago, and sat in the pit, with his hat drawn down over his eyes, studying elocution, and a ruffian recognized him. He had not his hat drawn enough down, and the ruffian called him out by name, "Rev. Mr. So-and-So," and called it with a blasphemy, and concluded by saying, "Let us pray!" The attention of the whole audience was directed to him. What was the matter? Why did he sit with his hat drawn down over his eyes? He was ashamed to be there. He had no business to be there. A vast incongruity in the case of any Christian man, when he sits in the theatre. The theatre as it now is, unwashed and polluted, is every day becoming more polluted; for I saw in some of the papers last night a statement of the fact that, in order to meet the pressure of these times, and more powerfully attract, the theatres are now presenting more indecent plays than ever. Oh, stand back from it, Christian men and women. Before God, this morning, promise your own soul, promise the Church of Christ, that you will never be seen in such places.

I can not let you go this morning until I

have said it is not all of life to live. We were not sent into the world merely for gayeties and amusements. Are you prepared for the great future? Hear you not the tolling of old Trinity and the tramp of the Seventh Regiment, and see you not the carrying out of the chief magistrate of our neighboring city? What does it all mean? A warning to the stout and the well; for he said, "I can endure any thing." This morning the sunlight gilds his grave! Oh, men of the strong arm, and of the stout chest, and of the swarthy development, "Be ye also ready; for in such an hour as ye think not, the Son of man cometh."

I was reading, just before I came to church this morning, of a woman who had gone all the rounds of sinful amusement, and she came to die. She said, "I will die to-night at six o'clock." "Oh," they said, "I guess not, you don't seem to be sick." "I shall die at six o'clock, and my soul will be lost. I know it will be lost. I have sinned away my day of grace." The noon came. They desired to seek religious counsel. "Oh no," she said, "it is of no use. My day is gone. I have been all the rounds of worldly pleasure, and it is too late. I shall die to-night at six o'clock, and my soul will be lost." The day wore away, and it came to four o'clock, and to five o'clock, and she cried out at five o'clock, "Destroyed spirits, ye shall not have me yet; it is not six, it is not six!" The moments went by, and the shadows began to gather, and the clock struck six; and while it was striking her soul went. What hour God will call for you I do not know—whether six o'clock to-night, or three o'clock this afternoon, or at one o'clock, or this moment. Sitting where you are, falling forward, or standing where you are, dropping down, where will you go to? I do not care what you came for; whether you came to approve, or came to denounce. I have you here now, and I want to tell you that Christ died for your immortal soul, and that if you will repent, you may be saved.

There were people who heard me preach last Sabbath morning about the theatre who were struck in the heart, and who during the past week have been inquiring the way to

God and to Heaven; and there are thousands of people in this audience who are just on the line between the right and the wrong, and I pray God that this may be the day of their disenthrallment. This moment choose Christ, and live.

CHRISTIAN GYMNASTICS.

"They that use this world, as not abusing it."—1 *Cor*. vii., 31.

MY text implies that there is a lawful use of the world as well as an unlawful abuse of it, and the difference between the man Christian and the man un-Christian is that in the former case the man masters the world, while in the latter case the world masters him. For whom did God make this grand and beautiful world? For whom this wonderful expenditure of color, this gracefulness of line, this mosaic of the ground, this fresco of the sky, this glowing fruitage of orchard and vineyard, this full orchestra of the tempest, in which the tree branches flute, and the winds trumpet, and the thunders drum, and all the splendors of earth and sky come clashing their cymbals? For whom did God spring the arched bridge of colors resting upon buttresses of broken storm-cloud? For whom did he gather the upholstery of fire around the window of the setting sun? For all men; but more especially for his own dear children.

If you build a large mansion, and spread a great feast after it to celebrate the completion of the structure, do you allow strangers to come in and occupy the place while you thrust your own children in the kitchen or the barn or the fields? Oh no. You say, "I am very glad to see strangers in my mansion, but my own sons and daughters shall have the first right there." Now God has built this grand mansion of a world, and he has spread a glorious feast in it; and while those who are strangers to his grace may come in, I think that God especially intends to give the advantage to his own children, those who are the sons and the daughters of the Lord Almighty, those who through grace can look up and say, "Abba Father." You can not make me believe that God gives more advantages to the world than he gives to the Church bought by his own blood. If, therefore, people of the world have looked with dolorous sympathy upon this host who have this day united with the Church, and have said, "Those new converts are going down into privation and into hardship. Why did not they tarry a little longer in the world, and have some of its enjoyments and amusements and recreations?" I say to such men of the world, "You are greatly mistaken," and before I get through I will show that those people who stay out of the kingdom of God have the hardships and self-denials, while those who come in have the joys and the satisfactions.

This morning, in the name of the King of heaven and earth, I serve a writ of ejectment upon all the sinful and polluted who have squatted on the domain of earthly pleasure as though it belonged to them, while I claim, in behalf of the good and the pure and the true, the eternal inheritance which God has given them.

Hitherto Christian philanthropists, clerical and lay, have busied themselves chiefly in denouncing sinful amusements; but I feel we have no right to stand before men and women in whose hearts there is a desire for recreation, amounting to positive necessity, denouncing this and that and the other thing, when we do not propose to give them something better. God helping me this morning, and with reference to my last account, I shall enter upon a sphere not usual in sermonizing, but a subject which I think ought to be presented at this time. I propose now to lay before you some of the amusements and recreations which are not only innocent, but positively helpful and advantageous.

In the first place, I commend, among indoor recreations, *music, vocal and instrumental.* Among the first things created was the bird, so that the earth might have music at the start. This world, which began with so sweet a serenade, is finally to be demolished amidst the ringing blast of the archangel's trumpet, so that as there was music at the start, there shall be music at the close. While this heavenly art has often been dragged into the uses of superstition and dissipation, we all know it may be the means of high moral culture. Oh, it is a grand thing to have our children brought up amidst the sound of cultured voices and amidst the melody of musical instruments.

There is in this art an indescribable fascination for the household. Let all those families who have the means to afford it, have flute or harp or piano or organ. As soon as the hand is large enough to compass the keys, teach it how to pick out the melody. Let all our young men try this heavenly art upon their nature. Those who have gone into it fully have found in it illimitable recreation and amusement. Dark days, stormy nights, seasons of sickness, business disasters, will do little toward depressing the soul which can gallop off over musical keys or soar in jubilant lay. It will cure pain. It will rest fatigue. It will quell passion. It will revive health. It will reclaim dissipation. It will strengthen the immortal soul. In the battle of Waterloo, Wellington saw that the Highlanders were falling back. He said, "What is the matter there?" He was told that the band of music had ceased playing, and he called up the pipers and ordered them to strike up an inspiriting air; and no sooner did they strike the air than the Highlanders were rallied, and helped win the day. Oh, ye who have been routed in the conflicts of life, try by the force of music to rally your scattered battalions.

I am glad to know that in our great cities there is hardly a night in which there are not concerts, where, with the best musical instruments and the sweetest voices, people may find entertainment. Patronize such entertainments when they are afforded you. Buy season tickets, if you can, for the "Philharmonic" and the "Handel and Haydn" societies. Feel that the dollar and a half or two dollars that you spend for the purpose of hearing an artist play or sing is a profitable investment. Let your Steinway Halls and your Academies of Music roar with the acclamation of appreciative audiences assembled at the concert or the oratorio.

Still further: I commend, as worthy of their support, *the gymnasium*. This institution is gaining in favor every year, and I know of nothing more free from dissipation, or more calculated to recuperate the physical and mental energies. While there are a good many people who have employed this institution, there is a vast number who are ignorant of its excellences. There are men with cramped chests and weak sides and despondent spirits who through the gymnasium might be roused up to exuberance and exhilaration of life. There are many Christian people despondent from year to year, who might, through such an institution, be benefited in their spiritual relations. There are Christian men who write hard things against their immortal souls, when there is nothing the matter with them but an incompetent liver. There are Christian people who seem to think that it is a good sign to be poorly; and because Richard Baxter and Robert Hall were invalids, they think that by the same sickliness they may come to the same grandeur of character. I want to tell the Christian people of my congregation that God will hold you responsible for your invalidism if it is your fault, and when through right exercise and prudence you might be athletic and well. The effect of the body upon the soul you acknowledge. Put a man of mild disposition upon the animal diet of which the Indian partakes, and in a little while his blood will change its chemical proportions. It will become like unto the blood of the lion or the tiger or the bear, while his disposition will change, and become fierce, cruel, and unrelenting. The body has a powerful effect upon the soul.

There are good people whose ideas of heaven are all shut out with clouds of tobacco-smoke. There are people who dare to shatter the physical vase in which God has put the jewel of eternity. There are men with great hearts and intellects in bodies worn out by their own neglects — magnificent machinery capable of propelling a *Great Eastern* across the Atlantic, yet fastened in a rickety North River propeller. Martin Luther was so mighty for God, first, because he had a noble soul, and secondly, because he had a muscular development which would have enabled him to thrash any five of his persecutors, if it had been Christian so to do. Physical development which merely shows itself in fabulous lifting, or in perilous rope-walking, or in pugilistic encounter, excites only our contempt; but we confess to great admiration for the man who has a great soul in an athletic body, every nerve, muscle, and bone of which is consecrated to right uses. Oh, it seems to me outrageous that men, through neglect, should allow their physical health to go down beyond repair, spending the rest of their life not in some great enterprise for God and the world, but in studying what is the best thing to take for dyspepsia! A ship which ought, with all sail set and every man at his post, to be carrying a rich cargo for eternity, employing all its men in stopping up leakages! When you may, through the gymnasium, work off your spleen and your querulousness and onehalf of your physical and mental ailments, do not turn your back upon such a grand medicament.

Still further: I commend to you a large class of *parlor games and recreations*. There is a way of making our homes a hundred-fold more attractive than they are now. Those parents can not expect to keep their children away from outside dissipations unless they make the domestic circle brighter than any thing they can find outside of it. Do not, then, sit in your home surly and unsympathetic, and with a half-condemnatory look, because of the sportfulness of your children. You were young once yourself; let your children be young. Because your eyes are dim and your ankles are stiff, do not denounce sportfulness in those upon whose eyes there is the first lustre, and in whose foot there is the bounding joy of robust health. I thank God that in our drawing-rooms and in our parlors there are innumerable games and sports which have not upon them the least taint of iniquity. Light up all your homes with innocent hilarities. Do not sit down with the rheumatism, wondering how children can go on so. Rather thank God that their hearts are so light, and their laughter is so free, and that their cheeks are so ruddy, and that their expectations are so radiant. The night will come soon enough, and the heart-break, and the pang, and the desolation—it will come soon enough for the dear children. But when the storm actually clouds the sky, it will be time enough for you to haul out your reef tackles. Carry, then, into your homes not only the innocent sports and games which are the inventions of our own day, but the games which come down with the sportfulness of all the past ages—chess and charades and tableaux and battledore and calisthenics, and all those amusements which the young people of our homes know so well how to contrive. Then there will be the parlor socialities—groups of people assembled in your homes, with wit and mimicry and joviality, filling the room with joy from the door to the mantel, and from the carpet to the ceiling. Oh, is there any exhilaration like a score of genial souls in one room, each one adding a contribution of his own individual merriment to the aggregation of general hilarity?

Suppose you want to go abroad in the city, then you will find the panorama and the art gallery—Schauss's and Snedecor's and Avery's exquisite collections of pictures. You will find the Metropolitan Museum and the Historical Society rooms full of rare curiosities, and scores of places which can stand plainly the test of the principles I have laid down in former discourses as to what is right and wrong in amusements. You will find the lecturing hall, which has been honored by the names of

Agassiz in natural history, Doremus in chemistry, Boynton in geology, Dr. Mitchell in astronomy, John B. Gough in moral reform, and scores and hundreds of men who have poured their wit and genius and ingenuity through that particular channel upon the hearts and consciences and imaginations of men, setting this country fifty years farther in advance than it would have been without the lecture platform.

I rejoice in the popularization of *outdoor sports*. I hail the croquet-ground and the fisherman's rod and the sportsman's gun. In our cities life is so unhealthy and unnatural that when the census-taker represents a city as having four hundred thousand inhabitants there are only two hundred thousand, since it takes at least two men to amount to one man, so depleting and unnerving and exhausting is this metropolitan life. We want more fresh air, more sunlight, more of the *abandon* of field-sports. I cry out for it in behalf of the Church of God as well as in behalf of secular interests. I wish that this winter our ponds and our rivers and our Capitoline

Grounds might be all aquake with the heel and the shout of the swift skater. I wish that when the warm weather comes the graceful oar might dip the stream, and the evening-tide be resonant with boatman's song, the bright prow splitting the crystalline billow. We shall have the smooth and grassy lawn, and we will call out people of all occupations and professions, and ask them to join in the ball-player's sport. You will come back from these outdoor exercises and recreations with strength in your arm, and color in your cheek, and a flash in your eye, and courage in your heart. In this great battle that is opening against the kingdom of darkness we want not only a consecrated soul, but a strong arm and stout lungs and mighty muscle. I bless God that there are so many recreations that have not on them any taint of iniquity; recreations in which we may engage for the strengthening of the body, for the clearing of the intellect, for the illumination of the soul.

There is still another form of recreation which I commend to you, and that is *the pleasure of doing good*. I have seen young men, weak and cross and sour and repelling in their disposition, who by one heavenly touch have wakened up and become blessed and buoyant, the ground under their feet and the sky over their heads breaking forth into music. "Oh," says some young man in the house to-day, "I should like that recreation above all others, but I have not the means." My dear brother, let us take an account of stock this morning. You have a large estate, if you only realized it. Two hands. Two feet. You will have, perhaps, during the next year at least ten dollars for charitable contribution. You will have twenty-five hundred cheerful looks, if you want to employ them. You will have five thousand pleasant words, if you want to speak them. Now what an amount that is to start with!

You go out to-morrow morning, and you see a case of real destitution by the way-side. You give him two cents. The blind man hears the pennies rattle in his hat, and he says, "Thank you, sir; God bless you." You pass down the street, trying to look indifferent; but you feel from the very depth of your soul a profound satisfaction that you made that man happy. You go on still farther, and find a poor boy with a wheelbarrow, trying to get it up on the curbstone. He fails in the attempt. You say, "Stand back, my lad; let me try." You push it up on the curbstone for him, and pass on. He wonders who that well-dressed man was that helped him. You did a kindness to the boy; but you did a great joy to your own soul. You will not get over it all the week.

On the street, to-morrow morning, you will see a sick man passing along. "Ah," you say, "what can I do to make this man happy? He certainly does not want money; he is not poor, but he is sick." Give him one of those twenty-five hundred cheerful looks that you have garnered up for the whole year. Look joy and hopefulness into his soul. It will thrill him through, and there will be a reaction upon your own soul. Going a little farther on, you will come to the store of a friend who is embarrassed in business matters. You will go in and say, "What a fine store you have! I think business will brighten up, and you will have more custom after a while. I think next spring will bring more prosperity to the country. Good-morning." You pass out. You have helped that young man, and you have helped yourself. And that night you go home; you sit by the fire, you talk a little, you sing a little, you laugh a little; you say, "I really don't know what is the matter with me. I never felt so splendidly in my life." I will tell what is the matter with you. You spent only two cents out of the ten dollars; you have contributed one out of twenty-five hundred cheerful looks; you have given ten, fifteen, or twenty of the five thousand pleasant words you are going to speak during the year; you have with your own hands helped the boy with the wheelbarrow, and you feel in body, mind, and soul the thrill of that recreation. Which do you think was the happier—Colonel Gardiner, who sat with his elbow on a table spread with all extravagant viands, looking off at a dog on the rug, saying, "How I would like to change places with him; I be the dog and he be Colonel Gardiner;" or those two Moravian missionaries who wanted to go into the lazaretto for the sake of attending the sick, and they were told, "If you go in there, you will never come out. We never allow any one to come out, for he would bring the contagion." Then they made their wills and went in, first to help the sick, and then to die. Which was the happier—Colonel Gardiner, or the Moravian missionaries dying for others? Was it all sacrifice when the missionaries wanted to bring the Gospel to the negroes at the Barbados, and, being denied the privilege, sold themselves into slavery, standing side by side, and lying side by side down in the very ditch of suffering, in order that they might bring those men up to life and God and heaven? Oh, there is a thrill in the joy of doing good! It is the most magnificent recreation to which a man ever puts his hand or his head or his heart.

But, before closing, I want to impress upon you that mere secular amusement and entertainment are not a fit foundation for your soul to build on. Have you never had in your own life illustrations of the fact that worldly amusements are not sufficient, and that the pleasures of this life are, after all, evanescent, and the morning that opens most brightly may end in the darkest night? I know there are those in this audience who seek in the pleasures of this world their chief satisfaction; and I want to tell them of the mistake they are making before they wake up in everlasting disappointment. I had an illustration in my own life of how evanescent is earthly pleasure, and how that which opens very brightly may end in darkness and gloom and trouble. I had read in books illustrations of the kind, but I never saw any that was as powerful as that which I had in my own life. Just after going to Philadelphia, and while I was yet ignorant of all the surroundings of that city, one Monday morning, fatigued somewhat with the duties of the previous Sabbath, I went out for the purpose of recreation, taking, in all, my wife, my only daughter, my elder sister Sarah, and her daughter, who was a young lady. It was a beautiful June morning. Passing along by the Schuylkill River, we saw some pleasure-boats waiting for excursionists; and one of our party said, "Suppose we take a row on the river." I said, "Well!" and in two minutes were all aboard—five of us in all. There had been a freshet some days before, and the stream was very violent. I laid hold the oars and pulled away, and there was laughter and shout and joy. Oh, it was a very gay party. I was pulling away with all my strength, when I heard a shout from the shore, and I saw a waving of the hand, as much as to say, "Stop! stop!" I looked back, and I saw we were within a few yards of the awful plunge over the dam—the dam that reaches across the Schuylkill. With a cry to God for help, and an agony that I can never describe, I laid on to the oars and tried to put back. It was too late. We went over with an awful plunge, the boat capsizing as we went. None of us being able to swim, we clung to the rim of the upset boat, save two—my wife, who was drawn under the dam instantly, and my child, who sank. From the shore very soon boats came, but it seemed like many hours. The survivors of the party got into the boat, and we looked around for the fairest and the best in all the group, but she was gone. And then I saw under the wave the straw-hat of my little child, and I clutched for it as with a death-grip, and I hauled her in, black with strangulation. There were five of us who first got into the boat, but there were only four of us who landed. For six days and nights the gunners stood firing the cannon across that river, the artillerymen expecting, by the disturbance of the air, to raise the body from the bottom of the river. They succeeded; but oh! what a change between that bright June morning when we went out with laughter and song, and that afternoon when we came across the Schuylkill Bridge in a close carriage, four of us; my half-dead and motherless child, wrapped in flannels, lying on my lap. Oh, God! upon such a bright morning, did there ever drop such a horrible night?

I learned a lesson that day which I teach this day to you, and that is, you ought not depend too much upon the pleasures and the amusements of this life. Oh, people of the world, learn this: that while the stream of earthly pleasure may break down into darkness and into death, the river of God's comfort and salvation flows on all through this world, emptying at last into the boundless, fathomless ocean of eternal joy. May God bring you this day into the soft and beautiful current! Only a few strokes of the oar, and you will be landed.

THEATRICAL INVASION OF THE SABBATH.

"Verily my Sabbaths ye shall keep."—*Exod.* xxxi., 13.

THE wisdom of cessation from hard labor one day out of the seven is almost universally acknowledged. The world has found out that it can do less work in seven days than in six, and that the fifty-two days of the year devoted to rest are an addition rather than a subtraction. Experiments have been made in all departments. The great Castlereagh thought he could work his brain three hundred and sixty-five days in the year, but after a while broke down and committed suicide; and Wilberforce said of him: "Poor Castlereagh! This is the result of the non-observance of the Sabbath." A celebrated merchant declared: "I should have been a maniac long ago but for the Sabbath." The nerves, the brain, the muscles, the bones, the entire physical, intellectual, and moral nature cry out for the Sabbatic rest. What is true of man is, for the most part, true of the brute. Travelers have found out that they come to their place of destination sooner when they let their horses rest by the way on the Sabbath. What is the matter with those forlorn creatures harnessed to some of our city cars? Why do they stumble and stagger and fall? It is for the lack of the Sabbatic rest. In other days, when the herdsmen drove their sheep and cattle from the Far West down to the seaboard, it was found out by experiment that those herdsmen and drovers who halted over the seventh day got down sooner to the seaboard than those who passed on without the observance of the holy Sabbath. The fishermen off the coast of Newfoundland declare that those men during the year catch the most fish who stop during the Lord's day. When I asked the Rocky Mountain locomotive engineer why he changed locomotives when it seemed to be a straight route, he said: "We have to let the locomotive stop and cool off, or the machinery would soon break down." Men who made large quantities of salt were told that if they allowed their kettles to cool over Sunday they would submit themselves to a great deal of damage. The experiment was made, some observing the Sabbath and some not observing the Sabbath. Those who allowed the fires to go down, and the kettles to cool once a week, were compelled to spend only a small sum for repairs; while in the cases where no Sabbath was observed many dollars were demanded for repairs. In other words, intelligent man and dumb beast and dead machinery cry out for the Lord's day.

While the attempt to kill the Sabbath by the stroke of axe and flail and the yard-stick has beautifully failed, it is proposed in our day to drown the Sabbath by flooding it with secular amusements. They would bury it very decently under the wreath of the target company, and to the music of all Strakosch's brazen instruments. There are to-day, in the different cities, ten thousand hands and ten thousand pens busy in attempting to cut out the heart of our Christian Sabbath, and leave it a mere skeleton of what it once was. The effort is organized and tremendous; and unless the friends of Christ and the lovers of good order shall rouse up right speedily, their sermons and their protests will be uttered after the castle is taken. There are cities in the land where the Sabbath has almost perished; and last Sabbath night New York was in full blaze of theatric and operatic entertainment; and it is becoming a practical question whether we who received a pure Sabbath from the hands of our fathers shall have piety and pluck enough to give to our children the same blessed inheritance. The eternal God helping us, we will!

I protest against this invasion of the holy Sabbath, in the first place, *because it is a war on Divine enactment.* God says, in Isaiah: "If thou turn away thy foot from doing thy pleasure on my holy day, thou shalt walk upon the high places." What did he mean by "doing thy pleasure?" He referred to secular and worldly amusements. A man told me he was never so much frightened as in the midst of an earthquake, when the beasts of the field bellowed in fear, and even the barnyard fowls screamed in terror. Well, it was when the earth was shaking and the sky was all full of fire that God made the great announcement: "Remember the Sabbath-day to keep it holy." Go along through the streets where the theatres are open on a Sabbath night; go up on the steps; enter the boxes of those places of entertainment, and tell me if that is keeping the Sabbath holy. "Oh," says some one, "God won't be displeased with a grand sacred concert." A gentleman who was present at a "grand sacred concert" last Sabbath night in one of the theatres of our great cities, said that during the exercises there were comic and sentimental songs, interspersed with coarse jokes; and there were dances, and a farce, and tight-rope walking, and a trapeze performance. I suppose it was a holy dance and a consecrated tight-rope. I am not certain, however, about that; but this I know, it was a "grand sacred concert."

We hear a great deal of talk about "the rights of the people" to have just such amusements on Sunday as they want to have. I wonder if the Lord has any rights. You rule your family, the Governor rules the State, the

President rules the whole land; I wonder if the Lord has a right to rule the nations and make the enactment, "Remember the Sabbath-day to keep it holy," and if there is any appeal to a higher court from that decision, and if the men who are warring against that enactment are not guilty of high treason against the Maker of heaven and earth. They have in our cities put God on trial. It has been the theatres and the opera-houses of the land plaintiffs, *versus* the Lord Almighty defendant, and the suit has been begun, and who shall come out ahead, you know. Whether it be popular or unpopular, I now announce it as my opinion that *the people have no rights save those which the great Jehovah gives them.* He has never given the right to man to break his holy Sabbath, and as long as his throne stands he never will give that right.

The prophet asks a question which I can easily answer, "Will a man rob God?" Yes. They robbed him last Sunday night at the theatres and the opera-houses, and I charge upon them the infamous and high-handed larceny. I believe with the sailor. The crew had been discharged from the vessel because they would not work while they were in port on the Lord's day. The captain went out to get sailors. He found one man, and he said to him, "Will you serve me on the Sabbath?" "No." "Why not?" "Well," replied the old sailor, "a man who will rob God Almighty of his Sabbath would rob me of my wages if he got a chance." Oh, it is dastardly mean when we break the Sabbath. Suppose you had seven oranges, and you gave to your child six of them, putting the other orange in your pocket for yourself, and you should find that the child had not been satisfied with the six oranges, and had come and stolen your seventh. That is precisely what men do when they break the Sabbath. Suppose you were poor, and you came to a dry-goods merchant and asked for some cloth for garments, and he should say, "I'll give you six yards," and while he was off from the counter binding up the six yards you should go behind the counter and steal one additional yard. That is what every man does when he breaks the Lord's Sabbath. God gives us six days out of seven, reserving one for himself, and you will not let him have it. It is mean beyond all computation.

Again: I am opposed to this desecration of the Sabbath by secular entertainments *because it is a war on the statutes of our State.* The law says:

"It shall not be lawful to exhibit, on the first day of the week, commonly called Sunday, to the public, in any building, garden, grounds, concert-room, or other room or place within the city and county of New York, any interlude, tragedy, comedy, opera, ballet, play, farce, negro minstrelsy, negro or other dancing, or any other entertainment of the stage, or any part or parts therein, or any equestrian, circus, or dramatic performance, or any performance of jugglers, acrobats, or rope-dancing."

Was there ever a plainer enactment than that? Who made the law? You, who at the ballot-boxes decided who should go to Albany and sit in the Legislature. They made the law for you and for your families; and now I say that any man who attempts to override that law insults you and me and every man

THE UNJUST JUDGE. 127

who has the right of suffrage in the State of New York. What have been the circumstances? The low manager of a low theatre in New York had an entertainment on a Sabbath night. The police came in and arrested him. The District Attorney did not, however, pursue the case. After a while the prominent leader of a prominent opera company advertises his entertainment. People of all professions and occupations protest against it. Judge Donohue comes along and issues an injunction forbidding the police in any wise to interfere with these Sabbath amusements. Judge Donohue says:

"I hereby order that the defendants, and each of them, their agents and servants, as well as the captains, sergeants, and officers of the Police Department of the city of New York, refrain from interrupting, or in any way interfering with any dramatic or operatic performance that plaintiff may arrange, give, or conduct at any of the theatres in the city of New York during any Sunday, and from arresting the plaintiff, or any other person or employé of the plaintiff aiding in such dramatic or operatic performance on Sunday for participating in such performance, and from interfering in any way or manner with the plaintiff's business as director of the Strakosch Italian Opera Company, an orchestral company, and a dramatic and operatic company performing on Sundays."

That injunction hovered over the city for three weeks, Judge Donohue meanwhile standing in defiance of the voters of New York, and of the State Legislature. Some say, as by quibble, it was necessary for him to entertain the motion, and to issue the injunction. Was it necessary for him for three weeks to be deciding this question? On Wednesday or Thursday the injunction was lifted. Alas! that it was not lifted sooner. What a pity it was that it took three whole weeks, during which secular amusements were trampling upon God's holy day, to find out that the Legislature of the State of New York have a right to forbid the opening of the theatres on the Lord's day!

Still further: I protest against this recent invasion of the Sabbath, *because it is a foreign war*. Now, if you heard at this moment the booming of a gun in the harbor, or a shell from some foreign frigate should drop into our streets, how long would you keep your seats in the Tabernacle? You would want to face the foe, and every gun that could be managed would be brought in use, and every ship that could be brought out of the Navy Yard would swing from her anchorage, and the question would be decided. You do not want a foreign war, and yet I have to tell you that this invasion of God's holy day is a foreign war. As among our own native-born population there are two classes — the good and the bad; so it is with the people who come from other shores — there are the law-abiding and the lawless. The former are welcome here. The more of them the better we like it. In this particular church there are representatives of all lands. I believe God intended our national heart to throb with the blood of all people! But let not the lawless come from other shores expecting to break down our Sabbath, and institute in the place of it a foreign Sabbath.

How do you feel, ye who have been brought

up amidst the hills of New England, about giving up the American Sabbath? Ye who spent your childhood under the shadow of the Adirondacks or the Catskills; ye who were born on the banks of the Tennessee or Ohio or Cumberland, how do you feel about giving up the American Sabbath? You say: "We shall not give it up. We mean to defend it, as long as there is left any strength in our arm or any blood in our heart!" Do not bring your Spanish Sabbath here; do not bring your Italian Sabbath here; do not bring your French Sabbath here; do not bring your German Sabbath here. It shall be for us and our children forever a pure, consecrated, Christian, American Sabbath.

I will make a comparison between the Sabbath as some of you have known it, and the Sabbath of Paris. I speak from observation. On Sabbath morning I was aroused in Paris by a great sound in the street. I said: "What is this?" "Oh," they said, "this is Sunday." An unusual rattle of vehicles of all sorts. The voices seemed more boisterous than on other days. People running to and fro, with baskets and bundles, to get to the rail-trains or gardens. It seemed as if all the vehicles in Paris, of whatever sort, had turned out for the holiday. The *Champs Elysées* one great mob of pleasure-seeking people. Balloons flying; parrots chattering; foot-balls rolling; peddlers hawking their knickknacks through the streets; Punch and Judy shows in a score of places, each one with a shouting audience; hand-organs, cymbals, and every kind of racket, musical and unmusical. When the evening came down, all the theatres were in full blare of music and full blaze of light. The wine stores and saloons were thronged with an unusual number of customers. At even-tide I stood and watched the excursionists coming home, fagged out men, women, and children, a Gulf Stream of fatigue, irritability, and wretchedness; for I should think it would take three or four days to get over that miserable way of Sundaying. It seemed more like an American Fourth of July than a Christian Sabbath.

Now, in contrast, I present one of the Sabbaths in one of our best American cities.

Holy silence coming down with the day dawn. Business men more deliberately looking into the faces of their children, and talking to them about their present and future welfare. Men sit longer at the table in the morning, because the stores are not to be opened, and the mechanical tools are not to be taken up. A hymn is sung. There are congratulation and good cheer all through the house. The streets silent until ten o'clock, when there is a regular, orderly tramp churchward. Houses of God, vocal with thanksgivings for mercies received, with prayers for comfort, with charities for the poor. Rest for the body. Rest for the soul. The nerves quieted, the temples cooled, the mind cleared, the soul strengthened, and our entire population turned out on Monday morning ten years younger, better prepared for the duties of this life, better prepared for the life that is to come. Which do you like best, the American Sabbath or the Parisian Sabbath? Do you know in what boat the Sabbath came across the seas and landed on our shores? It was in the *Mayflower*. Do you know in what boat the Sabbath will leave us, if it ever goes?

It will be in the ark that floats over a deluge of national iniquity.

Still further: I protest against this recent invasion of the Lord's day, *because it wrongs a vast multitude of employés of their rest.* The play actors and actresses can have their rest between their engagements; but how about the scene-shifters, the ballet-dancers, the call-boys, the innumerable attendants and supernumeraries of the American theatre? Where is their Sunday to come from? They are paid small salaries at the best. Alas for them! You see them on the stage in tinsel and tassel with halberds, or you see them in gauze whirling in toe tortures, and you mistake them for fairies or queens; but after twelve o'clock at night you may see them trudging through the streets in faded dress, shivering and tired, a bundle under their arms, seeking their homes in the garrets and cellars of the city. Now you propose to take from thousands of these employés throughout this country, not only all opportunity of moral culture, but all opportunity of physical rest. For God's sake, let the crushing Juggernaut stop at least one day in seven!

Again: I oppose this modern invasion of the Christian Sabbath *because it is a war on the spiritual welfare of the people.* You have a body? Yes. You have a mind? Yes. You have a soul? Yes. Which of the theatres on the Sabbath-day will give that soul any culture? I heard of a lady who came to enact a play on the boards of a Philadelphia theatre. Her conscience so wrought upon her while she stood there, that, instead of attending to the play, she sang,

> "Rock of Ages, cleft for me,
> Let me hide myself in thee."

It was a rare occurrence. Such things are not often witnessed or heard in the American theatre. Admitting that a man has a spiritual and immortal nature, which one of the theatres will culture it? Which one of the Sabbath performances in a theatre will remind men of the fact that unless they are born again they can not see the kingdom of God? Will the music of *La Grand Duchesse* help people at last to sing the song of the one hundred and forty and four thousand? Let the theatres of the country go on Sabbath after Sabbath for years, and in all that number of years how many Christians will they, under God, produce? Not one. Besides that, if you gentlemen of the theatre and the opera have six days in the week in which to exercise your evangelical and heavenly influence, ought you not to allow Christian institutions to have twenty-four hours? Is it unreasonable to demand that, if you have six days for the body and the intellect, we have one day at least for our immortal soul? Or, to put it in another shape, do you not really think that our imperishable soul is worth at least one-seventh as much as our perishable body? An artist has three gems — a cornelian, an amethyst, and a diamond. He has to cut them and to set them. Which one is he most particular about? Now, the cornelian is the body, the amethyst is the intellect, the diamond is the soul. For the two former you propose six days of opportunity, while you offer no opportunity at all for the last, which is in value as compared with the others like one hundred thousand million dollars to one farthing. Besides that, you must not forget that nine-tenths, ay, ninety-nine one-hundredths of all the Christian effort of this country are put forth on the Lord's day. That is the day in which the asylums and the hospitals and the prisons are visited by Christian men. That is the day when the youth of our country get their chief religious information. That is the day when the most of the charities are collected. That is the day when, under the blast of fifty thousand American pulpits, the sin of the land is assaulted and men are summoned to repent. When you make war upon any part of God's day, you make war upon the asylums, and the penitentiaries, and the hospitals, and the reform associations, and the homes of the destitute, and the Church of the living God, which is the pillar and the ground of the truth.

I am opposed to the invasion of the Sabbath, *because it is a war on our political institutions.* When the Sabbath goes down, the republic goes down. Men who are not willing to obey God's law in regard to Sabbath observance are not fit to govern themselves. Sabbath-breaking means dissoluteness, and dissoluteness is incompatible with self-government. What is the matter with republicanism in Italy and in Spain? No Sabbath. For ages they wanted a republic in France. After a while they got a republic; but one day Napoleon III., with his cavalry, rode through the streets, and down went the republic under the clattering hoofs. They have a republic there again; but every time a sick young man at Chiselhurst looks across the English Channel, the French government quakes from the Tuileries to Versailles. France never will have a permanent republic until she quits her roystering Sabbaths, and devotes one day in every week to the recognition of God and sacred institutions. Abolish the Sabbath, and you abolish your religious privileges. Let the bad work go on, and you have "the commune," and you have "the revolution," and you have the sun of national prosperity going down in darkness and blood. From that reign of terror may the God of Lexington and Gettysburg deliver us!

Still further: I am opposed to this invasion of the Sabbath *because it is unfair, and it is partial.* Why has it been during the past few weeks that some of the theatres have been allowed to be open and others not? Why not have all open? While some of the operas and theatres were open, some of our friends in the other theatres, although they were willing to bless society on Sunday with their dances and their farces, had to sit in their "greenrooms," chewing their beards, and "wasting their sweetness on the desert air."

Go further, and see how unfair it is. While operas and theatres in different cities are allowed to be open on the Sabbath-day, dry-goods establishments must be closed, and plumbing establishments, and the butcher's and the baker's, and the shoe-maker's and the hardware stores. Now tell me by what law of justice you compel me to shut the door of my store while you keep open the door of your theatre? Are the men and women connected with the theatrical profession so much better than other people, that you give them especial privilege? Are the ballet-girls better than the milliners? Are these men who stalk the stage, clutching bloody daggers and writing death-warrants with quills that have no ink in them, and manufacturing thunder with a Chinese gong—are they better than people who sell silks and harness and cutlery? Ladies and gentlemen of the theatre and opera, in what school did you get morals so far superior to all the rest of the people? May it please your honors, Judges of the Supreme Court, when you give to the opera and the theatre the right to be open on the Sabbath-day, you ought to give, at the same time, the right to all commercial establishments to be open, and to all mechanical establishments to be open. What is right in the one case is right in all the cases. But come now and be honest, you men who manage theatres and operas, and confess that you do not care any thing at all about the moral welfare of the people, but you only want more dollars. Indeed, the leader of one of the operas says in the public prints that unless he can have the theatre open on the Lord's day he can not afford to keep it running. We are told by the operatic and theatrical leaders that they must get money on Sabbath nights in order to pay the deficits of the other nights of the week.

Now, in answer to that I say that if men can not manage our theatres without breaking the Lord's day, they had better all go into bankruptcy together. We will never surrender our Christian Sabbath for the purpose of helping these violators pay their expenses. While there may be a difference of opinion among some people about the propriety of having theatricals during the week, I think all lovers of good order must unite in one solid, unanimous resistance to this infernal attempt to massacre the Christian Sabbath.

I congratulate our city that so far we have almost entirely escaped the invasion, and my confidence is in our mayor and our judges and our police officers that the laws of the State of New York will be executed. Above all, my confidence is in the good hand of God that has been over this city since its foundation. But I call this day upon all those who befriend Christian principles, and those who love our political freedom, to stand in solid phalanx in this Thermopylæ of our American history; for I believe as certainly as I stand here that the triumph or overthrow of American institutions depends upon this Sabbatic contest. Bring your voices, your pens, your printing-presses, and your pulpits into the Lord's artillery corps for the defense of our holy day. Decree before high Heaven that this war on your religious rights and the cradles of your children shall bring ignominious defeat to the enemies of God and the public weal. For those who die in the contest battling for the right we shall chisel the epitaph: "These are they who came out of great tribulation, and had their robes washed and made white in the blood of the Lamb." But for that one who shall prove in this moral crisis recreant to God and the Church there shall be no honorable epitaph. He shall not be worthy even of a burial-place in all this free land; but perhaps some steam-tug, at midnight, may carry out his poor remains and drop them in the sea, where the lawless winds which keep no Sunday will gallop over the grave of him who lived and died a traitor to God, the Church, and the free institutions of America. Long live the Christian Sabbath! Perish forever all attempts to overthrow it!

THE WHOLESALE SLAUGHTER.

"Who slew all these?"—2 *Kings* x., 10.

I SEE a long row of baskets coming up toward the palace of King Jehu. I am somewhat inquisitive to find out what is in the baskets. I look in, and I find the gory heads of seventy slain princes. As the baskets arrive at the gate of the palace, the heads are thrown into two heaps, one on either side the gate. In the morning the king comes out, and he looks upon the bleeding, ghastly heads of the massacred princes. Looking on either side the gate, he cries out, with a ringing emphasis, "Who slew all these?"

We have, my friends, lived to see a more fearful massacre. There is no use of my taking your time this morning in trying to give you statistics about the devastation and ruin and the death which strong drink has wrought in this country. Statistics do not seem to mean any thing. We are so hardened under these statistics that the fact that fifty thousand more men are slain, or fifty thousand less men are slain, seems to make no positive impression on the public mind. Suffice it to say, that intemperance has slain an innumerable company of princes—the children of God's royal family; and at the gate of the Church there are two heaps of the slain; and at the door of the household there are two heaps of the slain; and at the door of the legislative hall there are two heaps of the slain; and at the door of the university there are two heaps of the slain; and at the gate of this nation there are two heaps of the slain. When I look upon the desolation, I am almost frantic with the scene, while I cry out, "Who slew all these?" I can answer that question in half a minute. The ministers of Christ who have given no warning, the courts of law that have offered the licensure, the women who give strong drink on New-year's-day, the fathers and mothers who have rum on the sideboard, the hundreds of thousands of Christian men and women in the land who are stolid in their indifference on this subject—they slew all these!

Last Sabbath morning I talked to you about some of the modes by which drunkenness in this land was to be assaulted. I shall this morning come to a more specific subject, and tell you what I think are the sorrows and the doom of the drunkard, so that you to whom I speak may not come to the place of torment.

Some one says, "You had better let those subjects alone." Why, my brethren, we would be glad to let them alone if they would let us alone; but when I have in my pocket now four requests saying, "Pray for my husband, pray for my son, pray for my brother, pray for my friend, who is the captive of strong drink," I reply, we are ready to let that question alone when it is willing to let us alone; but when it stands blocking up the way to heaven, and keeping multitudes who are in the house of God this morning away from Christ and heaven, I dare not be silent, lest the Lord require their blood at my hands.

I think the subject has been kept back very much by the merriment people make over those slain by strong drink. I used to be very merry over these things, having a keen sense of the ludicrous. There was something very grotesque in the gait of a drunkard. It is not so now; for I saw in one of the streets of Philadelphia a sight that changed the whole subject to me. There was a young man being led home. He was very much intoxicated—he was raving with intoxication. Two young men were leading him along. The boys hooted in the street, men laughed, women sneered; but I happened to be very near the door where he went in—it was the door of his father's house. I saw him go up stairs. I heard him shouting, hooting, and blaspheming. He had lost his hat, and the merriment increased with the mob until he came up to the door, and as the door was opened his mother came out. When I heard her cry, that took all the comedy away from the scene. Since that time, when I see a man walking through the street, reeling, as I saw one last night, until he fell to the sidewalk here on Lafayette Avenue, the comedy is all gone, and it is a tragedy of tears and groans and heart-breaks. Never make any fun around me about the grotesqueness of a drunkard. Alas for his home!

The first suffering of the drunkard is in the *loss of his good name*. God has so arranged it that no man ever loses his good name except through his own act. All the hatred of men and all the assaults of devils can not destroy a man's good name, if he really maintains his integrity. If a man is honest and pure and Christian, God looks after him. Although he may be bombarded for twenty or thirty years, his integrity is never lost and his good name is never sacrificed. No force on earth or in hell can capture such a Gibraltar. But when it is said of a man, "He drinks," and it can be proved, then what store wants him for a clerk? what church wants him for a member? who will trust him? what dying man would appoint him his executor? He may have been forty years in building up his reputation—it goes down. Letters of recommendation, the backing up of business firms, a brilliant ancestry can not save him. The world shies off. Why? It is whispered all through the community, "He drinks; he drinks." That blasts him. When a young man loses his reputation for sobriety, he might as well be at the bottom of the sea. There are young men here who have their good name as their only capital. Your father started you out in city life. He could only give you an education. He gave you no means. He started you, however, under Christian influences. You have come to the city. You are now achieving your own fortune, under God, by your own right arm. Now look out, young man, that there is no doubt of your sobriety. Do not create any suspicion by going in and out of liquor establishments, or by any odor of your breath, or by any glare of your eye, or by any unnatural flush of your cheek. You can not afford to do it, for your good name is your only capital, and when that is blasted with the reputation of taking strong drink, all is gone. When I see the influences all around our young men to destroy them, I hardly know what to say. For the young men themselves, all compassion, and all sympathy. For the men who deal out the deadly stuff I have all pity, because they bring upon themselves the scorn of good society and the retribution of God; but for the liquor establishments themselves, and the rum-selling restaurants, may God Almighty consume them with the brightness of his coming!

Another loss which the inebriate suffers *is that of self-respect*. Just as soon as a man wakes up and finds that he is the captive of strong drink, he feels demeaned. I do not care how reckless he acts. He may say, "I don't care;" he *does* care. He can not look a pure man in the eye, unless it is with positive force of resolution. Three-fourths of his nature is destroyed; his self-respect gone; he says things he would not otherwise say; he does things he would not otherwise do. When a man is nine-tenths gone with strong drink, the first thing he wants to do is to persuade you that he can stop any time he wants to. He can not. The Philistines have bound him hand and foot, and shorn his locks, and put out his eyes, and are making him grind in the mill of a great horror. He can not stop. I will prove it. He knows that his course is bringing disgrace and ruin upon himself. He loves himself. If he could stop, he would. He knows his course is bringing ruin upon his family. He loves them. He would stop if he could. He can not. Perhaps he could three months or a year ago; not now. Just ask him to stop for a month. He can not; he knows he can not, so he does not try. I had a friend who for fifteen years was going down under this evil habit. He had large means. He had given thousands of dollars to Bible societies and reformatory institutions of all sorts. He was very genial and very generous and very lovable, and whenever he talked about this evil habit he would say, "I can stop any time." But he kept going on, going on, down, down, down. His family would say, "I wish you would stop." "Why," he would reply, "I can stop any time if I want to." After a while he had delirium tremens; he had it twice; and yet after that he said, "I could stop at any time if I wanted to." He is dead now. What killed him? Rum! Rum! And yet among his last utterances was, "I can stop at any time." He did not stop it, because he could not stop it. Oh, I want the young men of my congregation to realize the fact that there is a point in inebriation beyond which, if a man goes, he can not stop!

One of these victims said to a Christian man, "Sir, if I were told that I couldn't get a drink until to-morrow night unless I had all my fingers cut off, I would say, 'Bring the hatchet and cut them off now.'". I have a dear friend in Philadelphia, whose nephew came to him one day, and when he was exhorted about his evil habit, said, "Uncle, I can't give it up. If there stood a cannon, and it was loaded, and a glass of wine set on the mouth of that cannon, and I knew that you would fire it off just as I came up and took the glass, I would start, for I must have it." Oh, it is a sad thing for a man to wake up in this life and feel that he is a captive. He says, "I could have got rid of this once, but I can't now. I might have lived an honorable life and died a Christian death; but there is no hope for me now; there is no escape for me. Dead, but not buried. I am a walking corpse. I am an apparition of what I once was. I am a caged immortal, beating against the wires of my cage in this direction and in that direction; beating against the cage until there is blood on the wires and blood upon my soul, yet not able to get out. Destroyed without remedy!"

I go farther, and say that the inebriate suffers from *the loss of his usefulness*. Do you not recognize the fact that many of those who are now captives of strong drink only a little while ago were foremost in churches and in reformatory institutions? Do you not know that sometimes they knelt in the family circle? Do you not know that they prayed in public, and some of them carried around the holy wine on sacramental days? Oh yes, they stood in the very front rank; but they gradually fell away. And now, what do you suppose is the feeling of such a man as that, when he thinks of his dishonored vows and the dishonored sacrament, when he thinks of what he might have been and of what he is now? Do such men laugh, and seem very merry? Ah, there is, down in the depths of their soul, a very heavy weight. Do not wonder that they sometimes say strange things, and act very roughly in the household. You would not blame them at all, if you knew what they suffer. Do not tell such that there is no future punishment. Do not tell him there is no such place as hell. He knows there is. *He is there now!*

I go on, and say that the inebriate suffers from *the loss of physical health.* The older men in the congregation may remember that some years ago Dr. Sewell went through this country and electrified the people by his lectures, in which he showed the effects of alcohol on the human stomach. He had seven or eight diagrams, by which he showed the devastation of strong drink upon the physical system. There were thousands of people that turned back from that ulcerous sketch, swearing eternal abstinence from every thing that could intoxicate.

God only knows what the drunkard suffers. Pain files on every nerve, and travels every muscle, and gnaws every bone, and burns with every flame, and stings with every poison, and pulls at him with every torture. What reptiles crawl over his creeping limbs! What fiends stand by his midnight pillow! What groans tear his ear! What horrors shiver through his soul! Talk of the rack, talk of the Inquisition, talk of the funeral pyre, talk of the crushing Juggernaut—he feels them all at once. Have you ever been in the ward of the hospital where these inebriates are dying, the stench of their wounds driving back the attendants, their voices sounding through the night? The keeper comes up and says, "Hush, now, be still! Stop making all this noise!" But it is effectual only for a moment, for as soon as the keeper is gone they begin again, "Oh God! oh God! Help! help! Rum! Give me rum! Help! Take them off me! Take them off me! Oh God!" And then they shriek, and they rave, and they pluck out their hair by handfuls, and bite their nails into the quick, and then they groan, and they shriek, and they blaspheme, and they ask the keepers to kill them: "Stab me. Smother me. Strangle me. Take the devils off me!" Oh, it is no fancy sketch. That thing is going on in hospitals; ay, it is going on in some of the finest private residences in the city of Brooklyn to-day. It went on last night while you slept; and I tell you further that this is going to be the death that some of you will die. I know it. I see it coming.

Again: the inebriate suffers through *the loss of his home*. I do not care how much he loves his wife and children; if this passion for strong drink has mastered him, he will do the most outrageous things; and if he could not get drink in any other way, he would sell his family into eternal bondage. How many homes in our city have been broken up in that way no one but God knows.

Oh, is there any thing that will so destroy a man for this life and damn him for the life that is to come? I hate that strong drink. With all the concentred energies of my soul, I hate it. Do you tell me that a man can be happy when he knows that he is breaking his wife's heart, and clothing his children with rags? Why, there are on the streets of our city to-day little children, barefooted, uncombed, and unkempt—want on every patch of their faded dress, and on every wrinkle of their prematurely old countenance, who would have been in churches to-day, and as well clad as you are, but for the fact that rum destroyed their parents and drove them into the grave. Oh rum! thou foe of God, thou despoiler of homes, thou recruiting-officer of the pit, I hate thee!

But my subject takes a deeper tone, and that is, that the inebriate suffers *from the loss of the soul*. The Bible intimates that in the future world, if we are unforgiven here, our bad passions and appetites unrestrained, will go along with us and make our torment there. So that I suppose, when an inebriate wakes up in the lost world, he will feel an infinite thirst clawing on him. Now, down in the world, although he may have been very poor, he could beg or he could steal five cents with which to get that which would slake his thirst for a little while; but in eternity, where is the rum to come from? Dives could not get one drop of water. From what chalice of eternal fire will the hot lips of the drunkard drain his draught? No one to brew it. No one to mix it. No one to pour it. No one to fetch it. Millions of worlds then for the dregs which the young man just now slung on the saw-dusted floor of the restaurant. Millions of worlds now for the rind thrown out from the punch-bowl of an earthly banquet. Dives cried for water. The inebriate cries for rum. Oh, the deep, exhausting, exasperating, everlasting thirst of the drunkard in hell! Why, if a fiend came up to earth for some infernal work in a grog-shop, and should go back taking on its wing just one drop of that for which the inebriate in the lost world longs, what excitement it would make there! Put that one drop from off the fiend's wing on the tip of the tongue of the destroyed inebriate: let the liquid brightness just touch it; let the drop be very small, if it only have in it the smack of alcoholic drink; let that drop just touch the lost inebriate in the lost world, and he would spring to his feet and cry, "That is rum, aha! that is rum!" And it would wake up the echoes of the damned, "Give me rum! Give me rum! Give me rum!" In the future world I do not believe that it will be the absence of God that will make the drunkard's sorrow, I do not believe that it will be the absence of light, I do not believe that it will be the absence of holiness; I think it will be the absence of rum. Oh! "look not upon the wine when it is red, when it moveth itself aright in the cup, for at the last it biteth like a serpent, and it stingeth like an adder."

When I see establishments all round about us the influence of which is to destroy men for this life and the life that is to come, I feel sometimes indignant, sometimes humiliated. Sometimes one emotion is dominant, and sometimes another; but if you should ask me this morning, "What are you in favor of for the purpose of extirpating this evil?" I would say, I am ready for any thing that seems reasonable. You say, "Are you in favor of Sons of Temperance?" Yes. "Are you in favor of Good Templars?" Yes. "Are you in favor of Good Samaritans?" Yes. "Are you in favor of the Maine Liquor Law?" Yes. "Are you in favor of the women's movement at the West?" Yes. Yes. I think that if thirty women, baptized by the Holy Spirit, in the West, could drive out all the liquor from a village of one thousand inhabitants, then if we could have in this great city three thousand consecrated women (for in proportion as the castle is great and strong you must have troops), resolving to give themselves no peace until this crime was extirpated from the city, in six months three-fourths of the grog-shops would be gone. If there be three thousand women now in this city who will put their hands and their hearts to the work, I will take the contract for driving out all these moral nuisances from the city—at any rate three-fourths of them—in three months. If, when that host of three thousand consecrated women is marshaled, there be not one to lead them, then, as a minister of the Most High God, I will offer to take my position at the front of the host, and I will cry to them, "Come on, ye women of Christ, with your songs and your prayers! Some of you take the enemy's right wing, and some the left wing. Forward! The Lord of Hosts is with us; the God of Jacob is our refuge! Down with the dram-shops!"

But while I have been talking, last Sabbath and somewhat now, about the general evils, I want, in conclusion, to say one thing personal, for I do not like a sermon that has no personalities in it. Perhaps this has not had that fault already. I want to say, in the first place, to those who are the victims of strong drink, that while I declared some time ago that there was a point beyond which a man could not stop, I want to tell you that while a man can not stop in his own strength, the Lord God, by his grace, can help him to stop at any time.

Last summer I was in a room in New York where there were many men who had been reclaimed from drunkenness. I heard their testimony, and for the first time in my life there flashed out a truth I never understood. They said, "We were victims of strong drink. We tried to give it up, but always failed; but somehow, since we gave our hearts to Christ, he has taken care of us." I believe that the time will soon come when the grace of God will show its power here not only to save man's soul, but his body, and reconstruct, purify, elevate, and redeem it.

I verily believe that, although you feel grappling at the roots of your tongues an almost omnipotent thirst, if you will this morning give your heart to God he will help you, by his grace, to conquer. Try it. It is your last chance. I have looked off upon the desolation. Sitting under my ministry there are a good many people in awful peril; and, judging from ordinary circumstances, there is not one chance in five thousand that they will get clear of it. I see men in my congregation from Sabbath to Sabbath, my warm, personal friends, of whom I must make the remark that, if they do not change their course, within ten years they will, as to their bodies, lie down in drunkards' graves; and, as to their souls, lie down in a drunkard's perdition. I know that is an awful thing to say, but I can not help saying it. Oh, beware! You have not yet been captured. Beware! As you open the door of your wine-closet at noon to-day, may that decanter flash out upon you, "Beware!" and when you pour the beverage into the glass, in the foam at the top, in white letters, let there be spelled out to your soul, "Beware!" When the books of judgment are open, and ten million drunkards come up to get their doom, I want you to bear witness that I, this morning, in the fear of God, and in the love for your soul, told you, with all affection and with all kindness, to beware of that which has already exerted its influence upon your family, blowing out some of its lights — a premonition of the blackness of darkness forever. Oh, if you could only hear this morning Intemperance, with drunkards' bones, drumming on the head of the wine-cask the "Dead March" of immortal souls, methinks the very glance of a wine-cup would make you shudder, and the color of the liquor would make you think of the blood of the soul, and the foam on the top of the cup would remind you of the froth on the maniac's lip; and you would go home from this service and kneel down and pray God that, rather than your children should become captives of this evil habit, you would like to carry them out some bright spring day to Greenwood, and put them away to the last sleep, until at the call of the south wind the flowers would come up all over the grave — sweet prophecies of the resurrection. God has a balm for such a wound; but what flower of comfort ever grew on the blasted heath of a drunkard's sepulchre?

THE CRUSADE OF DEMONS.

[The Temperance League of Glasgow, Scotland, publish annually a New-year's Tract. The following was written at the solicitation of that society.]

NOT with the click and clang of glasses and decanters, but with the stroke of the bells of English chapel, Scotch kirk, and American church, all mingling in one chime, would we ring the old year out and the new year in. Putting the palm of my hand against the palm of yours, and clenching the fingers on the back part of the hand, and then jerking my arm backward so as to bring you a little farther over this way, I give you a warmhearted Christian grip, and wish you a Happy New-year.

I accept with pleasure the invitation of the Scottish Temperance League to write their annual tract, for I am by blood partly a Scotchman, have high cheek-bones, and am very stubborn when I think I am right. Now that the steamers are crowded with Scotchmen, Englishmen, and Irishmen coming to America, I must give a word of warning. Stop drinking before you come! Our climate and style of liquors soon swamp or kill your countrymen. Moderate drinkers in Britain soon become immoderate drinkers here. The same amount of rum that in your own country will make you exhilarant, will turn you into a gutter-inspector here. There is something in our climate to rush a man to ruin quicker, if he be on the wrong track. Besides that, I think we put more blue vitriol, potash, turpentine, copperas, and stramonium in our liquors than you do in yours. Oh, you ought to taste our Cognac and Old Otard! Some one declares the fondness of different nationalities for strong drink by saying, when Frenchman meets Frenchman, he takes wine; when German meets German, he takes beer; when Englishman meets Englishman, he takes ale; when Irishman meets Irishman, he takes whisky: but when American meets American, he takes the first thing he can lay his hands on. We have noticed that people of other lands coming here soon get our bad habits, and make quicker plunge than our own natives. Come, by all means! We want to see you—but leave your ale-pitcher at home.

Your land, like our own, swelters under the curse of strong drink, and it is time that we all take up arms against it. From the way men are everywhere mown down by this evil, it is evident that there must be a banded and organized effort against the world's sobriety. I think the original Liquor League was formed in the lower world. One day the bad spirits met together and resolved that our human race were too happy, and a delegation of four infernals was sent up to earth on embassy of mischief. One spirit said, "I will take charge of the vineyards!" Another said, "I will look after the grain-fields!" Another said, "I will supervise the dairy!" Another said, "I will take charge of the music!" They landed in the Great Sahara Desert, clutched their skeleton fingers in a handshake of fidelity, kissed each other good-bye with lip of blue flame, and separated for their mission.

The first spirit entered the vineyard one bright morning, and sat down on the twisted

THE VINEYARDS DESPOILED.

root of a grape-vine in sheer discouragement. He could not at first plan any harm for the vineyard. The clusters were so full and purple and luscious and pure. The air was fairly bewitched with their sweetness; health seemed to breathe from every ripened bunch. But in wrath at so much loveliness, the fiend grasped a cluster in his right hand, and squeezed it with utter hate, and lo! his hand was red with the liquid, and began to smoke. Then the fiend laughed, and said, as he looked at the crimson stream dripping from his hand, "That makes me think of the blood of broken hearts. I will strip the vineyard, and squeeze out all the clusters, and let the juices stand till they rot, and will call the process 'Fermentation.'" And a great vat was made, and men seeing it, brought cups and pitchers and dipped them, and went off, drinking as they went, till they dropped in long lines of death; so that when the fiend of the vineyards wanted to go back to his home in the pit, he trod on the bodies of the slain all the way, going down over a causeway of the dead.

The fiend of the grain-field waded chin-deep

through the barley and the rye. As he came in, he found all the grain talking about bread, and prosperous husbandmen, and thrifty homes. But the fiend thrust his long arms through the barley and rye, and pulled them up and flung them into the water, and kindled fires beneath by a spark from his own heart, and there was a grinding, and a mashing, and a stench. And men dipped their bottles into the fiery juice, and staggered, and blasphemed, and rioted, and fought, and murdered, till the fiend of the grain-field was so well pleased with their behavior, he changed his residence from the pit to a whisky-barrel; and there he sits by the door-way, at the bung-hole, laughing right merrily at the fact that out of so harmless a thing as barley and rye he has made this world a suggestion of Pandemonium.

The fiend of the dairy met the cows as they were coming up, full-uddered, from the pasture-field. As the maid milked, he said, "It will not take me long to spoil that mess. I will add to it some brandy and sugar and nutmeg, and stir them up into a milk-punch, and children will like it, and even temperance men will take it; and if I can do no more, I will make their heads ache, and hand them gradually over to the more vigorous fiends of the Satanic delegation." And then he danced a break-down on the shelf of the dairy till all the shining row of milk-pans quaked.

The fiend of music entered a grog-shop, and found the customers few. So he made circuit of the city, and gathered up all the instruments of sweet sound, and after the night had fallen he marshaled a band, and trombone blew, and cymbals clapped, and harp thrummed, and drum beat, and bugle called, and crowds thronged in and listened, and, with wine-cup in their right hand, began to whirl in a dance that grew wilder and stronger and rougher, till the room shook and the glasses cracked, and the floor broke through, and the crowd dropped into hell.

They had done their work so well, these fiends of vineyard and grain-field, and dairy, and concert-saloon, that, on getting back, high carnival was held, Satan from his throne announcing the fact that there was no danger of the earth's redemption so long as the vineyards and orchards and grain-fields and music paid such large tax to the diabolic. Then all the satyrs and spirits and demons cried Hear! hear! and, lifting their chalices of fire, drank "Long life to rum-sellers! Prosperity to the gallows! Success to the License Law!"

In view of the devastations of strong drink, my first word is to toilers of brain, or hand, or foot! God intended us all to be busy. The sun and the moon in six thousand years have rested only part of a day, and then it took a miracle to stop them. Nothing that God ever made, animate or inanimate, human or angelic, can afford to quit work. But the outlay of human energy often leads to inebriation. Men have so much to do that they think they must have artificial stimulus. Vast multitudes of professional men have found their nervous system exhausted, and their brain lethargic, and have resorted to this dangerous help. Now what a man can not do without perpetual stimulant I do not believe he ought to do. You are responsible for no more strength than that which you have in your arm, and for no more speed than you have in your foot, and for no more vivacity than you have in your brain. God asks no more, and the world has a right to expect no more. Notwithstanding this, some of the most brilliant men in the law and medicine, yea, even in the ministry, have fallen overboard. It will be a glorious day for Britain and the United States when all their professional men and artisans shall throw the bottle out of the back window. It may require a struggle; but what great and grand and glorious thing was ever done without a struggle? Let not the descendants of men who fell at Drumclog and Bothwell Bridge talk complainingly about sacrifices!

My next word is to parents! If I can persuade you that your present course of taking intoxicating liquor in the slightest, yea, in the ten-thousandth part of a risk, imperils your boys, you will knock out the end of your ale-keg, and pull out the corks of your wine-bottle, to let the beverage, which hitherto has made your lips smack, go into the ditch. You say you have never been harmed by it. Granted. But remember what I tell you this first day of

January, 1875. That if you proceed with your present idea about intoxicating liquors, the probability is your son John, or George, or Peter, or Henry, or James, or Frederick will break your heart with his dissipations. Do not let them be familiar with the odors of the wine-closet. Do not let them take the sugar from the bottom of the glass. Abstain not only for yourself, but for your children. Oh, father, if in the last hour of your life you can take the hand of your son and say, "Farewell! I thank God that I can trust my name and my property, and the defense of your mother in your keeping. I thank God that he ever gave me such a boy as you are!" in that hour you will be more than compensated for any self-sacrifice of appetite that you have made for his welfare. But suppose you should, on the other hand, come to stand at the death-couch of a dissipated son, and he should say, "I am lost! Father, you are to blame. You drank, and I thought you could do no wrong. But the habit which I learned in our sitting-room on winter nights at the entertainment of friends has been my destruction!" Ah! in such an hour a pile of beer-barrels high as heaven and deep as hell could not barricade your soul against remorse and chagrin unutterable.

My next word is to the fashionable and elegant! Beastly drunkenness is no temptation. But when intoxication fills its cut-glass or golden chalice under blazing chandelier and before flashing mirror, graceful gentlemen bowing to gay lady as they click the rim, then the thing is bewitching. Though the heavens fall, we must be in the fashion. The wedding-hour, when two immortals join their fate in holy alliance, and when, of all other occasions, hearts should be purest, yea, the wedding-hour has often been the starting-place of a dissipation which ended not until he who took the vows had fallen under the all-consuming influence of strong drink, and she who, among the throng of congratulating hearts, in clear, sweet voice promised, "I will!" had wandered out in the cold winter night, and from the abutment of a bridge looked down into the glassy water, and then, in hope of relief from earthly agonies, took a wild leap into the wave.

My last word is to temperance men of

Britain! To arms! I sound the tocsin of a war compared with which Sedan and Waterloo and Gettysburg were child's play. While we do not underrate the foe, let us not limit the power of the God in whose cause we have enlisted. The flag we bear is not stained with tears or blood. No skeletons will be found in the track of the host who march out for the defense of the right; but in the wake of this army of philanthropists will smile the harvests of reformed inebriates, and be heard the shout of children at the return of their fathers from the captivity of the wine-cup. "The mountains and the hills shall break forth into singing, and all the trees of the field shall clap their hands."

On the first day of January, some years ago, our Abraham Lincoln made proclamation of emancipation for all bondmen of my own country. Would God that on the first day of January, 1875, there might go forth in England, Scotland, and Ireland a proclamation of emancipation for all the slaves of strong drink! That would make the happiest of all happy New-years. God save the Queen! and give long life and peace to all her subjects!

THE AMERICAN PLAGUE-SPOT.

"Many of them also which used curious arts brought their books together, and burned them before all men; and they counted the price of them, and found it fifty thousand pieces of silver."—*Acts* xix., 19.

PAUL had been stirring up Ephesus with some lively sermons about the sins of that place. Among the more important results was the fact that the citizens brought out their bad books, and in a public place made a bonfire of them. I see the people coming out with their arms full of Ephesian literature and tossing it into the flames. I see an economist standing by, and hear him saying, "Stop this waste. Here are seven thousand five hundred dollars' worth of books; do you propose to burn them all up? If you don't want to read them yourselves, sell them, and let somebody else read them." "No," said the people, "if these books are not good for us, they are not good for any body else, and we shall stand and watch until the last leaf has turned to ashes. They have done us a world of harm, and they shall never do others harm." Hear the flames crackle and roar!

Well, my friends, one of the wants of the cities of this country is a great bonfire of bad books and newspapers. We have enough fuel to make a blaze two hundred feet high. Many of the publishing-houses would do well to dump into the blaze their entire stock of goods, and a great many of the newspaper establishments would do well to roll into the flames all their next issue of fifty or a hundred thousand copies. Bring forth the insufferable trash and put it into the fire, and let it be known in the presence of God and angels and men that you are going to rid your houses of the overtopping and underlying curse of a profligate literature.

The printing-press is the mightiest agency on earth for good and for evil. The minister of the Gospel standing in a pulpit has a responsible position, but I do not think it is as responsible as the position of an editor or a publisher. At what distant point of time, at what far out circle of eternity, will cease the influence of a Henry J. Raymond, or a Horace

Greeley, or a James Gordon Bennett? Take the simple statistic that our New York dailies now have a circulation of three hundred and fifty thousand per day, and add to it the fact that three of our weekly periodicals have an aggregate circulation of about one million, and then cipher, if you can, how far up, and how far down, and how far out, reach the influences of the American printing-press. Great God! what is to be the issue of all this? I believe the Lord intends the printing-press to be the chief means for the world's rescue and evangelization, and I think that the great last battle of the world will not be fought with swords or guns, but with types and presses—a purified and Gospel literature triumphing over, trampling down, and crushing out forever that which is depraved. The only way to fight a bad book is by printing a good one. The only way to overcome unclean newspaper literature is by scattering abroad that which is healthful. May God speed the cylinders of an honest, intelligent, aggressive Christian printing-press!

I have to tell you this morning that I believe that the greatest scourge that has ever come upon this nation has been that of unclean journalism. It has its victims in all occupations and departments. It has helped to fill insane asylums and penitentiaries and almshouses and dens of shame. The bodies of this infection lie in the hospitals and in the graves, while their souls are being tossed over into a lost eternity, an avalanche of horror and despair.

The London plague was nothing to it. That counted its victims by thousands, but this modern pest has already shoveled its millions into the charnel-house of the morally dead. Anthony Comstock has done a glorious work against an infamous literature. Let the people all do him honor. They tried the other night to kill him in Newark. If they had slain him in his battle against a bad literature, it would have kindled a fire of indignation that all the waters of the Hudson and the East River could not have extinguished. That man has already literally gathered up whole tons of iniquitous literature and consigned it to the flames. But the longest rail-train that ever ran over the Erie or Hudson tracks was not long enough or large enough to carry the beastliness and the putrefaction which have gathered up in the bad books and newspapers of this land in the last twenty years.

Now it is amidst such circumstances that I put this morning a question of overmastering importance to you and your families. What books and newspapers shall we read? You see I group them together. A newspaper is only a book in a swifter and more portable shape, and the same rules which will apply to book reading will apply to newspaper reading. What shall we read? Shall our minds be the receptacle of every thing that an author has a mind to write? Shall there be no distinction between the tree of life and the tree of death? Shall we stoop down and drink out of the trough which the wickedness of men has filled with pollution and shame? Shall we mire in impurity and chase fantastic will-o'-the-wisps across the swamps, when we might walk in the blooming gardens of God? Oh, no. For the sake of our present and everlasting welfare, we must make an intelligent and Christian choice.

Standing as we do chin-deep in fictitious literature, the first question that many of the young people are asking me, is: "Shall we read novels?" I reply, there are novels that are pure, good, Christian, elevating to the heart and ennobling to the life. But I have still further to say, that I believe that ninety-nine out of the one hundred novels in this day are baleful and destructive to the last degree. A pure work of fiction is history and poetry combined. It is a history of things around us with the licenses and the assumed names of poetry. The world can never pay the debt which it owes to such fictitious writers as Hawthorne, and Mackenzie, and Landor, and Hunt, and Arthur, and Marion Harland, and others whose names are familiar to all. The follies of high life were never better exposed than by Miss Edgeworth. The memories of the past were never more faithfully embalmed than in the writings of Walter Scott. Cooper's novels are healthfully redolent with the breath of the sea-weed and the air of the American forest. Charles Kingsley has smitten the morbidness of the world, and led a great many to appreciate the poetry of sound health, strong muscles, and fresh air. Thackeray did a grand work in caricaturing the pretenders to gentility and high blood. Dickens has built his own monument in his books, which are an everlasting plea for the poor and the anathema of injustice. Now I say books like these, read at right times and read in right proportion with other books, can not help but be ennobling and purifying; but, alas! for the loathsome and impure literature that has come upon this country in the shape of novels, like a freshet, overflowing all the banks of decency and common sense. They are coming from some of the most celebrated publishing houses of the country. They are coming with the recommendation of some of our religious newspapers. They lie on your centre-table to curse your children, and blast with their infernal fires generations unborn. You find these books in the desk of the school-miss, in the trunk of the young man, in the steamboat cabin, and on the table of the hotel reception-room. You see a light in your child's room late at night. You suddenly go in, and say, "What are you doing?" "I am reading." "What are you reading?" "A book." You look at the book; it is a bad book. "Where did you get it?" "I borrowed it." Alas! there are always those abroad who would like to loan your son or daughter a bad book. Everywhere, everywhere, an unclean literature! I charge upon it the destruction of ten thousand immortal souls, and I bid you this morning wake up to the magnitude of the theme. I shall take all the world's literature, good novels and bad, travels true and false, histories faithful and incorrect, legends beautiful and monstrous, all tracts, all chronicles, all epilogues, all family, city, State, National libraries, and pile them up in a pyramid of literature, and then I shall bring to bear upon it some grand, glorious, infallible, unmistakable Christian principles. God help me to speak with reference to the account I must at last render, and God help you to listen!

I charge you, in the first place, to stand aloof from all books *that give false pictures of human life*. Life is neither a tragedy nor a farce. Men are not all either knaves or heroes. Women are neither angels nor furies. And yet, if you depended upon much of the literature of the day, you would get the idea that life, instead of being something earnest, something practical, is a fitful and fantastic and extravagant thing. How poorly prepared are that young man and woman for the duties of to-day, who spent last night wading through brilliant passages descriptive of magnificent knavery and wickedness! The man will be looking all day long for his heroine in the tin shop, by the forge, in the factory, in the counting-room, and he will not find her, and he will be dissatisfied. A man who gives himself up to the indiscriminate reading of novels will be nerveless, inane, and a nuisance. He will be fit neither for the store, nor the shop, nor the field. A woman who gives herself up to the indiscriminate reading of novels will be unfitted for the duties of wife, mother, sister, daughter. There she is, hair disheveled, countenance vacant, cheeks pale, hands trembling, bursting into tears at midnight over the fate of some unfortunate lover. In the day-time, when she ought to be busy, staring by the half-hour at —nothing: biting her finger-nails to the quick. The carpet that was plain before will be plainer after having through a romance all night long wandered in tessellated halls of castles, and your industrious companion will be more unattractive than ever now that you have walked in the romance through parks with plumed princesses, or lounged in the arbor with the polished desperado. Oh, these confirmed novel readers! They are unfit for this life, which is a tremendous discipline. They know not how to go through the furnaces of trial where they must pass, and they are unfitted for a world where every thing we gain we achieve by hard, long-continuing, and exhaustive work.

Again, abstain from all those books which, while they have some good things about them, *have also an admixture of evil.* You have read books that had the two elements in them, the good and the bad. Which stuck to you? The bad! The heart of most people is like a sieve which lets the small particles of gold fall through, but keeps the great cinders. Once in a while there is a mind like a loadstone, which, plunged amidst steel and brass filings, gathers up the steel and repels the brass. But it is generally just the opposite. If you attempt to plunge through a hedge of burrs to get one blackberry, you will get more burrs than blackberries. You can not afford to read a bad book, however good you are. You say, "The influence is insignificant." I tell you that the scratch of a pin has sometimes produced the locked-jaw. Alas! if through curiosity, as many do, you pry into an evil book, your curiosity is as dangerous as that of the man who should take a torch into a gunpowder-mill, merely to see whether it really would blow up or not.

Only this last week, in a menagerie in New York, a man put his hand through the bars of a black leopard's cage. The animal's hide looked so sleek and bright and beautiful. He just stroked it once. The monster seized him, and he drew forth a hand torn and mangled and bleeding. Oh, touch not evil, even with the faintest stroke; though it may be glossy and beautiful, touch it not, lest you pull forth your soul torn and bleeding under the clutch of the black leopard. "But," you say, "how can I find out whether a book is good or bad without reading it?" There is always something suspicious about a bad book. I never knew an exception. Something suspicious in the index or the style of illustration. This venomous reptile almost always carries a warning rattle.

Again, I charge you to stand off from all those books *which corrupt the imagination and inflame the passions.* I do not refer now to that kind of a book which the villain has under his coat, waiting for the school to be out, and then, looking both ways to see that there is no policeman around the block, offers the book to your son on his way home. I do not speak of that kind of literature, but that which evades the law and comes out in polished style, and with acute plot sounds the tocsin that rouses up all the baser passions of the soul. Years ago a French lady came forth as an authoress under the assumed name of George Sand. She smokes cigars. She wears gentlemen's apparel. She steps off the bounds of decency. She writes with a style ardent, eloquent, mighty in its gloom, horrible in its unchastity, glowing in its verbiage, vivid in its portraiture, damning in its effects, transfusing into the libraries and homes of the world an evil that has not even begun to relent; and she has her copyists in all lands. To-day, under the nostrils of your city, there is a fetid, reeking, unwashed literature, enough to poison all the fountains of public virtue and smite your sons and daughters as with the wing of a destroying angel, and it is time that the ministers of the Gospel blew the trumpet and rallied the forces of righteousness, all armed to the teeth in this great battle against a depraved literature.

Again, abstain from those books which are *apologetic of crime.* It is a sad thing that some of the best and most beautiful book-bindery and some of the finest rhetoric has been brought to make sin attractive. Vice is a horrible thing anyhow. It is born in shame, and it dies howling in the darkness. In this world it is scourged with a whip of scorpions, but afterward the thunders of God's wrath pursue it across a boundless desert, beating it with ruin and woe. When you come to paint carnality, do not paint it as looking from behind embroidered curtains or through lattice of royal seraglio, but as writhing in the agonies of a city hospital. Cursed be the books that try to make impurity decent, and crime attractive, and hypocrisy noble! Cursed be the books that swarm with libertines and desperadoes, who make the brain of the young people whirl with villainy! Ye authors who write them, ye publishers who print them, ye booksellers who distribute them, shall be cut to pieces, if not by an aroused community, then at last by the aid of divine vengeance, which shall sweep to the lowest pit of perdition all ye murderers of souls. I tell you, though you may escape in this world, you will be ground at last under the hoof of eternal calamities, and you will be chained to the rock, and you will have the vultures of despair clawing at your soul, and those whom you have destroyed will come around to torment you, and to pour hotter coals of fury upon your head, and rejoice eternally in the outcry of your pain and the howl of your damnation. "God shall wound the hairy scalp of him that goeth on in his trespasses."

The clock strikes midnight. A fair form bends over a romance. The eyes flash fire. The breath is quick and irregular. Occasionally the-color dashes to the cheek, and then dies out. The hands tremble as though a guardian spirit were trying to shake the deadly book out of the grasp. Hot tears fall. She laughs with a shrill voice that drops dead at its own sound. The sweat on her brow is the spray dashed up from the river of death. The clock strikes "four," and the rosy dawn soon after begins to look through the lattice upon the pale form that looks like a detained spectre of the night. Soon in a mad-house she will mistake her ringlets for curling serpents, and thrust her white hand through the bars of the prison, and smite her head, rubbing it back as though to push the scalp from the skull, shrieking, "My brain! my brain!" Oh, stand off from that. Why will you go sounding your way amidst the reefs and warning buoys, when there is such a vast ocean in which you may voyage, all sail set?

There is one other thing I shall say this morning before I leave you, whether you want to hear it or not; that is, that I consider the lascivious pictorial literature of the day as most tremendous for ruin. There is no one who can like good pictures better than I do. The quickest and most condensed way of impressing the public mind is by picture. What the painter does by his brush for a few favorites the engraver does by his knife for the million. What the author accomplishes by fifty pages the artist does by a flash. The best part of a painting that costs ten thousand dollars you may buy for ten cents. Fine paintings belong to the aristocracy of art. Engravings belong to the democracy of art. You do well to gather good pictures in your home. Spread them before your children after the tea-hour is past, and the evening circle is gathered. Throw them on the invalid's couch. Strew them through the rail-train to cheer the traveler on his journey. Tack them on the wall of the nursery. Gather them in albums and port-folios. God speed the good pictures on their way with ministries of knowledge and mercy.

But what shall I say of the prostitution of this art to purposes of iniquity? These death-warrants of the soul are at every street-corner. They smite the vision of the young with pollution. Many a young man buying a copy has bought his eternal discomfiture. There may be enough poison in one bad picture to poison one soul, and that soul may poison ten, and the ten fifty, and the hundreds thousands, until nothing but the measuring-line of eternity can tell the height and depth and ghastliness and horror of the great undoing. The work of death that the wicked author does in a whole book the bad engraver may do on half a side of a pictorial. Under the disguise of pure mirth the young man buys one of these sheets. He unrolls it before his comrades amidst roars of laughter, but long after the paper is gone the result may perhaps be seen in the blasted imaginations of those who saw it. The Queen of Death every night holds a banquet, and these periodicals are the printed invitation to her guests. Alas! that the fair brow of American art should be blotched with this plague-spot, and that philanthropists bothering themselves about smaller evils should lift up no united and vehement voice against this great calamity!

Young man! Buy not this moral strychnine for your soul! Pick not up this nest of coiled adders for your pocket! Patronize no news-stand that keeps them! Have your room bright with good engravings, but for these outrageous pictorials have not one wall, not one bureau, not one pocket. A man is no better than the pictures he loves to look at. If your eyes are not pure, your heart can not be. By a news-stand one can guess the character of a man by the kind of pictorial he purchases. When the devil fails to get a man to read a bad book, he sometimes succeeds in getting him to look at a bad picture. When Satan goes a-fishing, he does not care whether it is a long line or a short line, if he only draws his victim in.

Beware of lascivious pictorials, young man; in the name of Almighty God, I charge you.

If I have this morning successfully laid down any principles by which you may judge in regard to books and newspapers, then I have done something of which I shall not be ashamed on the day which shall try every man's work, of what sort it is. Cherish good books and newspapers. Beware of the bad ones. One column may save your soul; one paragraph may ruin it. Benjamin Franklin said that the reading of Cotton Mather's "Essay to Do Good" moulded his entire life. The assassin of Lord Russell declared that he was led into crime by reading one vicious romance. The consecrated John Angel James, than whom England never produced a better man, declared, in his old days, that he had never yet got over the evil effects of having for fifteen minutes once read a bad book. But I need not go so far off. I could come nearer home, and tell you of something that occurred in my college days. I could tell you of a comrade who was great-hearted, noble, and generous. He was studying for an honorable profession, but he had an infidel book in his trunk, and he said to me one day, "De Witt, would you like to read it?" I said, "Yes, I would." I took the book and read it only for a few minutes. I was really startled with what I saw there, and I handed the book back to him, and said, "You had better destroy that book." No, he kept it. He read it. He re-read it. After a while he gave up religion as a myth. He gave up God as a nonentity. He gave up the Bible as being a fable. He gave up the Church of Christ as a useless institution. He gave up good morals as being unnecessarily stringent. I have heard of him but twice in many years. The time before the last I heard of him he was a confirmed inebriate. The last time I heard of him he was coming out of an insane asylum — in body, mind, and soul an awful wreck. I believe that one infidel book killed him for two worlds.

Go home to-day and look through your library, and then, having looked through your library, look on the stand where you keep your pictorials and newspapers, and apply the Christian principles I have laid down this morning. If there is any thing in your home that can not stand the test, do not give it away, for it might spoil an immortal soul; do not sell it, for the money you get would be the price of blood; but rather kindle a fire on your kitchen hearth or in your back yard, and then drop the poison in it, and keep stirring the blaze until, from Preface to Appendix, there shall not be a single paragraph left, and the bonfire in Brooklyn shall be as consuming as that one in the streets of Ephesus.

So you see I have resumed the series of sermons I have been preaching on Sabbath mornings in regard to public iniquities. I shall go on. Next Sabbath morning I shall talk to you, if God spares my life, about the God-defying extravagance of our American cities, and on the following Sabbath morning about the perils of an unclean life. I will have you understand that I have only plowed one furrow of a whole field, which I mean yet, if God helps me, to turn up. I am encouraged in this series of sermons by the letters which I have received from all parts of this land, north, south, east, and west; by the testimony of young men who say they have changed their course of life; by the thanks of parents, who say that their families have been reconstructed on some of the principles of Christian ethics that have been laid down. Yes, I have been encouraged by the approval of my own conscience, and the assurance that I have in this matter been favored of God. Yes, I have been encouraged by the agitation in the enemy's camp; for when I see such a great scattering among the troops, I know the bombshell struck. So I shall go on. I know some of my enemies say, as Goliath said to little David, "Come to me, and I will give thy flesh unto the fowls of the air, and to the beasts of the field." But I reply to that in the words of David to the Philistine, "Thou comest to me with sword, and spear, and shield: but I come to thee in the name of the Lord of hosts, the God of the armies of Israel, whom thou hast defied. This day will the Lord deliver thee into mine hand, that all the earth may know that there is a God in Israel."

Professor Vandenhoff covered up this city with advertisements, "Vandenhoff *versus* Talmage." He first demolished me in Brooklyn, in the Academy of Music, and two nights after he demolished me in Steinway Hall, New York. In the audience-room of our beautiful Academy of Music, which holds three thousand people, he had, on a clear night, a beggarly attendance of two hundred and fifty. That was his first demolishing. Then he went to New York, and in a vast hall that holds between two and three thousand people, had another audience of two hundred and fifty. This was the second time he demolished me. He is out of pocket some five or six hundred dollars, I am told. Poor man! I am sorry for him. If he will come to me I will help pay the deficit. But he has shown to all this country that in our great cluster of cities, with more than a million population, there can be got together only five hundred people on the side of immorality, and against the Church of the Son of God. Be encouraged, all Christian people. The brothels will go down. The grog-shops will go down. The theatres will go down. You and I may not live to see the consummation of all our wishes, but the cause of God is marching on in the world, and organized iniquity shall perish, and the throne of righteousness shall be established in all the earth. "Blessed be the Lord God of Israel, from everlasting to everlasting, and let the whole earth be filled with His glory. Amen, and Amen."

GOD-DEFYING EXTRAVAGANCE OF MODERN SOCIETY.

"Moreover the Lord saith, Because the daughters of Zion are haughty, and walk with stretched forth necks and wanton eyes, walking and mincing as they go, and making a tinkling with their feet: in that day the Lord will take away the bravery of their tinkling ornaments about their feet, and their cauls, and their round tires like the moon, the chains, and the bracelets, and the mufflers, the bonnets, and the ornaments of the legs, and the head-bands, and the tablets, and the ear-rings, the rings, and nose-jewels, the changeable suits of apparel, and the mantles, and the wimples, and the crisping-pins, the glasses, and the fine linen, and the hoods, and the veils."—*Isaiah* iii., 16, 18–23.

THROUGH this window of the text we look in upon the voluptuousness of an ancient city—the description, with a very little variation, as appropriate to New York and Brooklyn as to Jerusalem and Tyre. One might think that Isaiah had before him the fashion-plates, and the head-dresses, and the jewel-caskets, and the dancing-schools, and the drawing-room parties of the present day, and that he foresaw Saratoga and Brighton and

Long Branch. Through this same window of the text we also see the masculine extravagance and dissipation which always correspond with the feminine. Woman may have greater varieties of apparel, but she lives a quieter life and therefore, may have the great varieties and luxuries of dress without impediment. Men would wear as much, if they knew how without interfering with their worldly occupations. The rough jostling of life is inimical to a man's dragging a dress-trail two yards in length, or pending from his ear a diamond cluster. In the time of the text, as well as in all ages of the world, the two sexes were alike in moralities or immoralities.

While in parlor sentimentalities it is well that men defer to women, and women defer to men, in the presence of God, and in the light of eternal responsibilities, the sexes are equal.

Our text takes us twenty-five hundred years back, and sets us down in an ancient city. It is a bright day, and the ladies are all out. The procession of men and women is moving up and down the gay streets. It is the height of the fashionable season. The sensible people

JERUSALEM FASHIONABLES.   199

move with so much modesty that they do not attract our attention. But here come the haughty daughters of Jerusalem! They lean forward; they lean very much forward: so far forward as to be unnatural—teetering, wobling, wriggling, flirting, or, as my text describes it, they "walk with stretched forth necks, walking and mincing as they go." They have spent hours before the mirror ere starting from home, and have in most astounding style arranged their bonnets and their veils and their entire apparel, and now go through the streets, taking more of the pavement than they are entitled to, sweeping along with skirts that the text describes as "round tires like the moon." See! that is a princess! Look! that is a Damascus sword-maker! Look! that is a Syrian merchant! The jingling of the chains, and the flashing of the head-bands, and the exhibitions of universal swagger attract the attention of the prophet Isaiah, and he brings his camera to bear upon the scene, and takes a picture for all the ages. But where is that scene? Vanished. Where are those gay streets? Vermin-covered population pass through them. Where are the hands, and the necks, and the foreheads, and the shoulders, and the feet that sported all that magnificence? Ashes! Ashes!

Taking my text as a starting-point, this morning I come out to talk to you about the God-defying extravagance of modern society. For the refinements and the elegances and adornments of life, I cast my vote. While I was thinking over this subject, there was handed into my house a basket of flowers, paradisiacal in their beauty. White calla, with a green background of bergonia; heliotropes nestling among geraniums; sepal, corolla, and perianth showed the touch of God's fingers. In the snow of the camelia, in the fire-dye of the rose, in the sky-blue of the English violet, I learned that God loves adornment. He might have made this earth so as to satisfy the gross demands of sense, but left it without adornment or attraction. Instead of the variegated colors of the seasons, the earth might have worn a dress of unchanging dull brown. The trees might have put forth their fruit without the prophesy of leaf or blossom. Niagara might have let down its waters in gradual descent without thunder and winged spray. But no. Look out, on some summer morning, after a heavy night-dew, and see whether or not God loves jewels. Put a snow-flake under a microscope, and see whether God does not love exquisite architecture. He decreed that the breastplate of the priest in olden time should have a wreath of gold, and the hem of his garment should be worked into figures of pomegranate. When the world sleeps, God blankets it with the brilliants of the night sky, and when it wakes, he washes it in the burnished laver of the sunrise.

But it is absolutely necessary that we draw a line between that which is the lawful use of beautiful adornment and that extravagance which is the source of so much crime, wretchedness, and abomination in our day. That is sinful extravagance when you go into any thing beyond your means. That which is right for one may be wrong for another. That which is lawful expense for a queen may be sinful outlay for a duchess. That which may be economy for you with larger income may be squandering for me with smaller income. But when men and women cross over the line which separates between what they can pay for, and still keep a sufficiency to meet moral obligation on the one hand, and, on the other hand, that extravagance which one's means can not compass, they have passed from the innocent into the culpable. Across that line have gone "a multitude that no man can number."

We judge of what we ought to have by what other people have. If they have a sumptuous table, and fine residence, and gay turn-out, and exquisite apparel, and brilliant surroundings, we must have them irrespective of our capacity to stand the expense. We throw ourselves down in despair because other people have a seal-skin coat, and we have an ordinary one; because others have diamonds, and we have garnets; because others have Axminster, and we have Brussels; because others have lambrequins, and we have plain curtains. What others have we mean to have anyhow. So there are families hardly able to pay their rent, and in debt to every merchant in the neighborhood, who sport apparel inapt for their circumstances, and run so near the shore that the first misfortune in business, or the first besiegement of sickness tosses them into pauperism. There are thousands of families moving from neighborhood to neighborhood, staying long enough in each one to exhaust all their capacity to get trusted. They move away because the druggists will give them no more medicine, and the butchers will afford them no more meat, and the bakers will give them no more bread, and the grocers will furnish them with no more sugar until they pay up. Then they suddenly find out that the neighborhood is unhealthy, and they hire a cartman, whom they never pay, to take them to a part of the city where all the druggists and butchers and bakers and grocers will be glad to see them come in, and sending to them the best rounds of beef, and the best coffee, and the best of every thing, until the slight suspicion comes into their brain that all the pay they will ever get from their customer is the honor of his society! There are about five thousand such thieves in Brooklyn. You see I call it by a plain name, because when a man buys a thing that he does not expect to pay for he is a thief.

There are circumstances where men can not meet their obligations. It is as honest for some men to fail as it is for other men to succeed. They do their best, and through the misfortunes of life they are thrown, and they can not pay their debts. That is one thing; but when you go and purchase an article for which you know there is no probability of your ever making recompense, you are a villain! Why do you not save the time of the merchant and the expense of an accountant for him? Why do you not go down some day to his store, and, when no one is looking, shoulder the ham or the spare-rib, and in modest silence take them along with you? That would be a lesser crime; for now you get not only the merchant's goods, but you get his time, and you rouse up his expectations. If you must steal, steal so it will be the least possible damage to the trader. John Randolph arose in the American Senate, and, stretching himself up to full height, cried out, with a shrill voice, "Mr. Chairman, I have found the philosopher's-stone that turns every thing into gold: Pay as you go."

My friends, society has to be reconstructed on this subject. You have no right to ride in a carriage when you owe the wheelwright who furnished the landau, and the horse-dealer who provided the blooded span, and the harness-maker who caparisoned the gay steeds, and the livery-man who furnished the stabling, and the driver who sits with rosetted hat on your coach-box. I am glad to see you ride. The finer your horses and the better your carriage the better it pleases me. But if you are in debt for the equipage, and hopelessly in debt, get down and walk like the rest of us! It is well to understand that it is not the absolute necessities that we find it so hard to meet, but the fictitious wants. God promises us shelter, but not a palace; and raiment, but not chinchilla; and food, but not canvas-back duck. As long as we have enough to meet the positive necessities of life, we ought to be content until we can afford the superfluities. As soon as you see a man deliberately consent that his outgo shall exceed his income, you may know he has started on the broad road to bankruptcy and moral ruin.

This wholesale extravagance accounts for a great deal of depression in national finances. Aggregates are made up of units, and so long as one-half of the people of this country are in debt to the other half, you can not have a healthy financial condition. The national resources are drawn off, not only for useless extravagances, but for those that are positively pernicious. The theatres of New York cost that city every year two millions of dollars. We spend in this country ninety-five millions of dollars every year for cigars and tobacco. In the United States we expend annually one thousand four hundred and eighty-three millions of dollars for rum. Now, take those facts, and is it strange that our national finances are crazied? If you have an exportation of breadstuffs four times what you have now, and an importation of gold four times what you have now, there would be no permanent prosperity in this country until people quit their sinful lavishment, and learn honest economy. You charge it upon Salmon P. Chase, or Boutwell, or Secretary Richardson. I charge it upon you, the men and women who are living beyond your means.

This wide-spread extravagance also accounts for much of the crime. It is the source of many abscondings, bankruptcies, defalcations, and knaveries. The store on Broadway and the office on Wall Street are swamped by the residence on Madison Square. The husband and father has his craft capsized because he carries too much sail of point-lace and Antuilly guipure. That is what destroyed Ketcham, and Swartwout, and ten thousand men not so famous. That is what springs the leak in the merchant's money-till, and pulls down your trust companies, and cracks the pistols of your suicides, and halts this nation on its high career of prosperity. I arraign this monster of extravagance in the sight of all the people, and ask you to pelt it with your scorn and denounce it with your anathema.

This wide-spread extravagance also accounts for much of the pauperism in the country. Who are the individuals and the families who are thrown on your charity? Who has sinned against them so that they suffer? It is often the case that their parents, or their grandparents, had all luxuries, lived every thing up, more than lived every thing up, and then died, leaving their families in want. The grandparents of these beggars supped on Burgundy and woodcock. There are a great many families who have every luxury in life, yet expend every dollar that comes in, and perhaps a few dollars more, not even taking the common Christian prudence of having their lives insured. While they live all is well, but when they die their children are pitched into the street. I tell you a man has no right to die under such circumstances. His death is a grand larceny. If a man has been industrious and economical, and has not a farthing to leave his children as he goes away from them, he has a right to put them in the hands of the Father of the fatherless and know they will be cared for; but if you, with every comfort in life, are lavish and improvident, and then depart this life leaving your children to be hurled into pauperism, you deserve to have your bones sold to the medical museum for anatomical specimens, the proceeds to furnish your children bread. I know the subject cuts close. I expected that some of you in high dudgeon would get up and go out. You stand it pretty well. Some of you are making a great swosh in life, and after a while will die, leaving your families beggars, and you will expect us ministers of the Gospel to come and stand by your coffin, and lie about your excellences; but we will not do it. If you send for me, I will tell you what my text will be: "He that provideth not for his own, and especially for those of his own household, is worse than an infidel."

In this day, God has mercifully allowed those of us who have limited income to make provision for our families, through the great life-insurance companies all over the land. By some self-denial on our part, we can make this provision for those whom we shall leave behind us. Is there any thing so helpless as a woman whose husband has just died, when, with her children at her back, she goes out in this day to fight for bread? Shall she become a menial servant in some one else's household?

No; not the one that has been lying on your arm all these years, and filling the household with joy and light. Shall she sew for a living? God knows that they get but six cents and eight cents for making one garment. Ah no! you had better have your coffin made large enough to take them all with you into that land where they never freeze nor starve. How a man with no surplus of estate, but still enough money to pay the premium on a life-insurance policy, can refuse to do it, and then look his children in the face, and say his prayers at night on going to bed, expecting them to be answered, is a mystery to me that I have never yet been able to fathom.

This extravagance is becoming more and more wide-spread. A statistician has estimated that there are in New York and Brooklyn four thousand five hundred women who expend annually two thousand dollars each in dress. It is no rare thing, when the wedding march sounds, to see dragging through the aisle a bridal dress that has cost its thousand or fifteen hundred dollars. Things have come to such a pass that, when we cry over sin, we wipe the tears away with a hundred-and-fifty-dollar pocket-handkerchief. The tendency to extravagance was illustrated wonderfully when the late James Fisk, Jun., sent the bridal presents to the home of William M. Tweed, a gentleman now occupying apartments at government expense. Fisk sent an iceberg of frosted silver, polar bears of silver lying down on the handles, polar bears of silver walking over the gold spoons. There were in the house that day forty silver sets of imperial magnificence. There was a diamond set that cost forty-five thousand dollars. There was one dress that had in it thirty-seven yards of silk, with three hundred and eighty-two bows. Hundreds of thousands of dollars expended on that scene. The reason we have not a multitude of scenes as extravagant is because we have not so much money.

This wicked extravagance shows itself no more forcibly than on the funeral day. No one else seems willing to speak of it, so I shall speak of it. There has been many a man who has died solvent, but has been insolvent before he got under the ground. One would think that the two debts most sacred would be debts to the physician and the undertaker, since they are the last two debts contracted; and yet those two professions are swindled more frequently than any other. In the agitation and excitement the friends come, and they want extraordinary attention, and they want extraordinary expenditure, and then, when the sad scene is past, neglect to make compensation. What are those two professions to do under such circumstances? If a merchant sells goods, and they are not paid for, I understand he can reclaim the goods; but if a man departs this life, and, through his friends, indebtedness is contracted that is not met, there seems to be no relief, for the patient has gone off with the doctor's pills and the undertaker's white slippers. Greenwood and Laurel Hill and Mount Auburn hold to-day thousands of such swindlers. A man dies in our neighboring city of New York. He has lived a fictitious life, moved amidst splendor, and dies leaving his family not a dollar; but they, poor things! must keep up the same magnificence, and so they resolve upon a great funeral. The obsequies shall be splendid! I give you no imaginary case. I give you the funeral of a man in up-town New York life, the facts authenticated, and in my pocket. The undertaker was not to blame; he only sold them what they asked for. The only blame was for those who bought when they knew they could not pay.

Casket, covered with Lyons velvet, silver mouldings......	$850
Heavy plated handles...	60
Solid silver plate, engraved in Roman letters................	75
Ten linen scarfs...	150
Floral decorations...	225
Music and quartette choir at the house..........................	40
Twenty carriages, walking to the cemetery.....................	140
Then fifteen other important expenditures, amounting to	336
All the expenditures, added up, being.......................	$1876

for getting one poor mortal to his last home! Perhaps it would have been all well if they had been able to meet the expenditure; but when it was known they could not, it was a villainy. There are families that you know who, in the effort to meet the ridiculous, outrageous, and wicked customs of society in regard to obsequies, have actually reduced themselves to penury. They put their last dollar in the ground. They wanted bread, and you gave them a stone.

There is in England what they call a funeral reform. It is high time we had such a reform society in our own country.

This wide-spread extravagance accounts, also, for the poverty of religious institutions. Men pay so much for show they have nothing for God and religion. We pay in this country twenty-two millions of dollars for the great benevolent societies; but what are the twenty-two millions of dollars compared with the ninety-five millions for cigars and tobacco, and the one thousand four hundred and eighty-three millions for drink? How do you like the comparison?

My friends, let us set ourselves in battle array against this God-defying extravagance. Buy not those things which are frivolous, when you may after a while be in lack of the necessities. Buy not books you will never read, nor pictures you will never study. Put not a whole month's wages into one trinket. Keep your credit good by seldom or never asking for any. Pay. Starve not a whole year so as to be able to afford one Belshazzar's carnival. Do not buy a coat of many colors, and then in six months be out at the elbows. Do not pay so much for a muffler for the neck, and be almost barefooted. Flourish not, as some I know of, in elegant hotels with drawing-room apartments, and then vanish in the night, not even leaving your compliments for the landlord.

In the great day of fire, we will have to give an account not only for how we made our money but for how we spent it. On this cold day, when so many are suffering, and there is want before us and want behind us and want on either side of us, let us quit our waste. Men and women of God, I call upon you to set a Christian example. Remember that soon you will have to leave your wardrobe and equipage. I do not want you to feel on that day like the dying actress, who ordered up her casket of jewels, and then with her pale, dying hand rolled them over, and said, "Alas! that I must give you up so soon." In that day, better have one treasure in heaven, just one, than to have had the bridal trousseau of a Queen

Maria Louisa, or to have sat with Caligula at a banquet which cost four hundred thousand dollars, or to have been carried out in a pageant, with senators and princes for pall-bearers. They who consecrate to God their time, their talents, and their all, shall be held in everlasting remembrance, while the name of the wicked shall rot.

THE SHEARS OF DELILAH.

"And she called for a man, and she caused him to shave off the seven locks of his head; and she began to afflict him, and his strength went from him."—*Judges* xvi., 19.

IT would take a skillful photographist to picture Samson as he really was. The most facile words are not supple enough to describe him. He was a giant, and a child; the conqueror, and the defeated; able to snap a lion's jaw, and yet captured by the sigh of a maiden. He was ruler, and slave; a commingling of virtues and vices, the sublime and the ridiculous; sharp enough to make a good riddle, and yet weak enough to be caught in the most superficial stratagem; honest enough to settle his debt, and yet outrageously robbing somebody else to get the material to pay it; a miracle, and a scoffing; a crowning glory, and a burning shame.

There he stands, looming up above other men, a mountain of flesh; his arms bunched with muscle that can lift the gate of a city;

taking an attitude defiant of armed men and wild beasts. His hair had never been cut, and it rolled down in seven great plaits over his shoulders, adding to his fierceness and terror. The Philistines want to conquer him, and therefore they must find out where the secret of his strength lays. There is a woman living in the valley of Sorek by the name of Delilah. They appoint her the agent in the case. The Philistines are secreted in the same building, and then Delilah goes to work and coaxes Samson to tell what is the secret of his strength. "Well," he says, "if you should take seven green withes, such as they fasten wild beasts with, and put them around me, I should be perfectly powerless." So she binds him with the seven green withes. Then she claps her hands, and says, "They come—the Philistines!" and he walks out as though there were no impediment. She coaxes him again, and says, "Now tell me the secret of this great strength;" and he replies, "If you should take some ropes that have never been used, and tie me with them, I should be just like other men." She ties him with the ropes, claps her hands, and shouts, "They come —the Philistines!" He walks out as easy as he did before—not a single obstruction. She coaxes him again, and he says, "Now, if you should take these seven long plaits of hair, and by this house-loom weave them into a web, I could not get away." So the house-loom is rolled up, and the shuttle flies backward and forward, and the long plaits of hair are woven into a web. Then she claps her hands, and says, "They come—the Philistines!" He walks out as easily as he did before, dragging a part of the loom with him. But after a while she persuades him to tell the truth. He says, "If you should take a razor, or shears, and cut off this long hair, I should be powerless, and in the hands of my enemies." Samson sleeps, and, that she may not wake him up during the process of shearing, help is called in.

You know that the barbers of the East have such a skillful way of manipulating the head, to this very day, that, instead of waking up a sleeping man, they will put a man, wide awake, sound asleep. I hear the blades of the shears grinding against each other, and I see the long locks falling off. The shears, or razor, accomplishes what green withes and new ropes and house-loom could not do. Suddenly she claps her hands, and says, "The Philistines be upon thee, Samson!" He rouses up with a struggle, but his strength is all gone! He is in the hands of his enemies! I hear the groan of the giant as they take his eyes out, and then I see him staggering on in his blindness, feeling his way as he goes on toward Gaza. The prison-door is opened, and the giant is thrust in. He sits down and puts his hands on the mill-crank, which, with exhausting horizontal motion, goes day after day, week after week, month after month—work, work, work! The consternation of the world in captivity, his locks shorn, his eyes punctured, grinding corn in Gaza!

Alas! for those fatal shears. They did the work, and they have kept on doing the work. They have not yet finished their mission. Those shears are busy to-day cutting off not only the locks of Samson, but also of Delilah.

It seems to me that it is high time that pulpit and platform and printing-press speak out against the impurities of modern society. Fastidiousness and Prudery say, "Better not speak; you will rouse up adverse criticism; you will make worse what you want to make better; better deal in glittering generalities; the subject is too delicate for polite ears." But there comes a voice from Heaven overpowering the mincing sentimentalities of the day, saying, "Cry aloud, spare not, lift up thy voice like a trumpet, and show my people their transgressions, and the house of Jacob their sins." So that, turning away from the advice of men, I take counsel of God, and this day arraign, expose, and denounce the impurities of modern society.

The trouble is that when people write or speak upon this theme they are apt to cover it up with the graces of *belles-lettres*, so that the crime is made attractive instead of repulsive. Lord Byron in *Childe Harold* adorns this crime until it smiles like a May-queen. Michelet, the great French writer, covers it up with passionate rhetoric, until it glows like the rising sun. Before I get through, you will find that I am not making that mistake, for instead of making this crime, so prevalent in modern society, attractive, I shall make it as loathsome as a small-pox hospital.

There are to-day influences abroad which, if unresisted by the pulpit and the printing-press, will turn New York and Brooklyn into Sodom and Gomorrah, fit only for the storm of fire and brimstone that whelmed the cities of the plain. You who are seated in your Christian homes, compassed by moral and religious restraints, do not realize the gulf of iniquity that bounds you on the north and the south and the east and the west; but I shall this day open the door of ghastliness and horror, and compel you to see and compel you to listen until, God helping, you shall be startled and aroused, throwing out one arm for help and the other arm for battle. While I speak, there are tens of thousands of men and women going over the awful plunge of an impure life; and while I cry to God for mercy upon their souls, I call upon you to marshal in the defense of your homes, your church, and your nation.

There is a banqueting-hall that you have never heard described. You know all about the feast of Ahasuerus, where a thousand lords sat. You know all about Belshazzar's carousal, where the blood of the murdered king spirted into the faces of the banqueters. You may know of the scene of riot and wassail when there was set before Esopus one dish of food that cost four hundred thousand dollars. But I speak to-day of a different banqueting-hall. Its roof is fretted with fire. Its floor is tessellated with fire. Its chalices are chased with fire. Its song is a song of fire. Its walls are buttresses of fire. It is the banqueting-hall of a libertine's and adulteress's perdition. Solomon refers to it when he says, "Her guests are in the depths of hell."

I shall this morning explain to you how so often the shears of destruction come upon the locks of Samson and Delilah. Beginning on the lower round, I have to tell you that *pauperism is the cause of a great deal of the uncleanness.* There are many people in our midst who have to choose between the almshouse and crime. There are women who can get neither sewing nor any other kind of work. What are they to do? What shall become of them? Thousands and tens of thousands of them have been fighting the battle for bread five, ten, fifteen years. They sold the piano, they sold the pictures, they sold the library, they sold the carpet, they sold the chairs, they sold the bed, they sold the wardrobe; there is one thing more to sell, and that is their immortal nature. At that crisis infamous solicitation meets them, and they go down. With one awful fling they throw away their needle and their soul.

Besides this, there are in this cluster of cities—and when I say in this sermon this cluster of cities, I mean New York, Jersey City, and Brooklyn—there are in this cluster of cities six hundred thousand people who are jammed together in tenement-houses, with no opportunity for seclusion or decency, and do you wonder that so many of them forget the covenant of their God? Forty and fifty families sometimes, literally forty and fifty families, crowded together under one roof. One hundred and seventy thousand families living in twenty-seven thousand houses—this tenement-house outrage more terrible than any thing to be found in all Christendom, putting out of sight almost the London stories of St. Giles and Whitechapel. These tenement-houses are the hopper for the mill that is grinding up the bodies and the souls of men, women, and little children. Some time ago a girl of fourteen years came into one of the reform schools in New York. The teacher of the school said, "Poor girl, did you forget your mother, and that it was a sin?" She looked up and said, "No, I didn't forget my mother. My mother has no clothes, and I have no shoes, and this dress is almost worn out, and the winter's coming on. I know what it is to make money, sir. Why, I have taken care of myself since I was ten years of age. You think it was a sin, do you?" And the tears rolled down her face, and she did not try to wipe them away. "It was a sin, but I didn't ask you to forgive me. Men can't forgive, but God can. I know, sir, what men are. The rich do wickedness, but nothing is said about them. But I am poor, and God knows that many a time I have gone hungry all day because I didn't dare to spend a penny or two —all I had left. Oh, sir, I sometimes wish that I could die. I wonder why God don't kill me." Alas! for the poor things. Do you wonder that they go down? Moral: do all you can for the poor. Keep them from being crowded off into sin. Snuff not up the idea in derision that any body should surrender to such temptations. There are sitting before me to-day five hundred people in furs and diamonds who, under the same pressure, would have gone overboard! If, oh man, oh woman, you have not done as badly as they, it is because you have not been as much tempted. If Delilah has not shorn your locks, it is because she has not had the same chance at you.

Again I remark, that *the corrupt literature of this day is the cause of much uncleanness.* I referred to this in a former sermon, but I reserved to this day some facts which will appall you. You know that there are hundreds of thousands of sheets in the shape of impure novelette literature going abroad, every plot of those novelettes turning on libertinism and full of salacious suggestion. Much of the printing-press of the country reeks with pollution. The child that comes to fifteen or sixteen years of age now in these cities has read more bad books and seen more bad pictures than your grandmother and grandfather read or saw up to the time they put on spectacles. There was one citizen in Brooklyn who made four hundred thousand dollars by publishing obscene books, and when he was seized by Governmental authority there was found thirty thousand dollars' worth of stock on hand. That man is dead, and gone to perdition; but his wife has his money, and now moves, I am told, in respectable circles. It must be told that of the four men who originally published all the obscene books and newspapers in this country, three of them lived in Brooklyn. Two of them are dead, thank God! I wish they all were.

In the city of New York there was one house under the control of a man who was a member of the church, and that house did nothing but make bad books, circulars, and pictures. When the authorities seized upon the place, they found whole tons of stereotyped plates for doing nothing but the printing of bad circulars and books. That man was a member of the church. He was awfully pious! He had on the mantel in his factory a rack containing religious tracts, with the inscription on the outside, "Take one." I do not know whether to this day he has been excommunicated, for other churches have not the moral courage which the Session of this church had when, last spring, finding a bad man in our membership, they unanimously ejected him, all the sixteen men of the Session having the moral daring to vote "Ay." God speed the day when it shall be impossible for a man to practice iniquity and yet keep his place in the membership of a Christian church!

But to go back to my theme. There was one man in our neighboring city who published and sold to one dealer one hundred and twenty-five thousand obscene books. When the authorities came upon him there were found forty thousand copies yet unsold. Binding these bad books in one of the factories were forty young women. One hundred and ninety thousand obscene photographs and engravings have been arrested in their flight of death. Twenty tons of iniquitous literature have been thrown into the flames. But the tide of evil goes on. How many are engaged in it? Some with the title of M. D. at the end of their names, implying themselves public benefactors and friends of humanity.

These people despoil the souls of men and women, if not in one way, then in another. They send their circulars and handbills far away. They put their infamous pictures on the back of playing-cards. They cut them into watch-cases. The venders in this business have the names of all the boarding-schools in the country, male and female, and not only the names of all the schools, but the names of all the students. The catalogues have been found in possession of these vultures, and their circulars and their pictures and their books go through the Post-office Department to all the young. The base circulars and advertisements are thrown into your door-way. They are flinging across this land the plagues of Egypt, the frogs and the boils and the murrain and the lice, turning the rivers into blood and the heavens into darkness. You, the father and mother, do not know it; but your children come to fifteen or sixteen years of age have seen the pictures and have read the books. There is not a school, not a shop, not a factory, not a home but has been assaulted in some way by this literature. So far from exaggerating the evil, if you could to-day understand the magnitude of it, it seems to me you would rise up from your seats and shriek out with horror. These villains—be they authors, engravers, publishers, or venders—ought to be seized of the law, summarily tried, sentenced to the full extent of the statute, and on swiftest express train hurried up to Sing Sing Penitentiary; and no man found in gubernatorial or presidential chair should ever dare to pardon one of them. This evil does not need the snail-pace of the law; it wants the quick spring of human and divine indignation.

Again: *Infidelity and skepticism* are the two blades of a shears which clip off much of the purity of the land. I do not mean to say that all skeptics are themselves unclean, but I do say that they open one of the widest doors to this iniquity. Purity and the sanctity of the marriage relation have only one foundation, and that is this book which King James got fifty-four ministers to translate, and which Robert Barker first printed in English. You throw away your Bible, and you throw away chastity and the marriage relation. A man that fights against that book fights in behalf of licentiousness. Infidelity is the mother of Fourierism, Communism, Mormonism, Socialism, Free-loveism, and much of what is falsely called "Woman's Rights." I abhor the whole herd of them. There are many rights that belong to woman which I hope in some day will be accorded to her; but I tell you, my Christian brethren, this whole subject of "Woman's Rights" in our day is so mixed up with infidelity and lust that you had better, if you are decent people, come off that platform, and let the maniacs have it all to themselves. We propose to build a Christian platform, on which we shall discuss the rights of both sexes, as God in his Word lays down those rights. I charge upon Free-loveism that it has blighted innumerable homes, and that it has sent innumerable souls to ruin. Free-loveism is bestial; it is worse — it is infernal. It has furnished this land with about five hundred divorces annually. In one county in the State of Indiana it furnished eleven divorces in one day before dinner. It has roused up elopements north, south, east, and west. You can hardly take up a paper but you read of an elopement.

As far as I can understand the doctrine of Free-loveism, it is this: that every man ought to have somebody else's wife, and every wife somebody else's husband! They do not like our Christian organization of society, and I wish they would all elope, the wretches of one sex taking the wretches of the other, and start to-morrow morning for the great Sahara Desert, until the simoon shall sweep seven feet of sand over all of them, and not one passing caravan for the next five hundred years bring back one miserable bone of their carcasses. Free-loveism! It is the double-distilled extract of nux vomica, ratsbane, and adder's-tongue. Free-loveism has raised in this city of Brooklyn a stench that has gone all over the world, and I think they will have to shut up the windows and gates of heaven to keep out the insufferable mal-odor. Never, until society goes back to the old Bible, and hears its eulogy of purity and its anathema of uncleanness, never until then will the fatal shears be unriveted.

Again: *The American theatre is the cause of much impurity.* It has debauched the nation. The play-actors and the play-actresses for the most part are licentious people. The exceptions to it are as rare as " four-leafed clovers." My conscience smites me when I think of the sermons I have been preaching about the theatre, in the fact that I have not half stated the uncleanness and the rottenness of that institution. Take the most denunciatory things I have said, and add to them fifty per cent. of Christian indignation, and then you will not come up to the truth. Most houses have a side-door and a back-door, as well as a front-door. I tell you the front-door of the house of shame in this day is the theatre. When you go there, in nine cases out of ten you put yourselves under lascivious influences, you put your feet in the footsteps of those who have gone down the whole stairs of iniquity. You may be pure now; but if you do not go just as far as they have gone, it will not be because you are more prudent, but because the grace of God miraculously saves you. Oh, beware of this institution, against which the Church of God and the best people in society are set in battle array! I hereby offer a reward of five hundred dollars to any body who will during this week send me the name of any one who is eminent for piety, and at the same time advocates and frequents the American theatre as it now is. Gentlemen of the press will please to get that just right.

An institution which has for its support play-actors, the majority of whom are unclean, the plays and literature of which are unclean, and that is favored and honored by all the unclean of earth—an institution like that must be a door to uncleanness. Take your head out of the lap of that infamous Delilah; she will cut your locks off.

Again: *The evil solicitation of the street* shears off much of the moral strength. The uncleanness under the gas-light of the street-lamp may disgust you, but it is an appalling fact that night by night there are thousands going down under the process. Solomon a good many years ago gave a picture of Broadway and the Bowery after nine o'clock at night: "She sitteth at the door of her house, on a seat in the high places of the city, to call passengers who go right on their ways: whoso is simple, let him turn in hither; and as for him that wanteth understanding, she saith to him, Stolen waters are sweet, and bread eaten in secret is pleasant. But he knoweth not that the dead are there."

Twenty-five hundred of those lost souls trudging the streets in this cluster of cities night by night on their errand of death! Hovering around hotels and dépôts! Flaunting their insignia of iniquity! Laughing the fiend's laugh! Rolling up and down in surges of death! Twenty-five hundred taking down their victims! New York pre-eminent above all the cities in this land for this infamy! One of the superintendents of police declared that there were enough houses of iniquity in New York to make a line three miles long, and that they would crowd Broadway from the Battery to Houston Street, in solid blocks, on each side;

some of them having all the repulsions of Arch Block and of the sailors' boarding-house, but some having all the glitter of the Fifth Avenue parlor. Upholstery outflaming the setting sun; mirrors winged with cherubim; fountains trickling mid-room into aquariums afloat with bright fins; pictures that rival the Louvre and Luxembourg; carpets embracing the feet with their luxuriance; Chickering grand pouring out upon the night-air snatches of opera to charm passers-by. But the dead are there; and if the enchanter's wand could be only turned backward, or inverted, the upholstery would turn into a shroud, and the bright fountain into waters ropy and scummed, and the chandelier into the fretted roof of a sepulchre, and the song into a dirge, and the gay denizens of the place into the wan faces of the damned.

These places are all the time being filled up by the tides that are coming in from the villages and the cities around us — ay, from the beautiful houses of this city, pouring in and falling down into an aggregation of misery and suffering inexpressible. Nine-tenths of the inmates are the victims of man's profligacy, and are now taking their vengeance on society: reaching up from the depths of their souls' suicide, clutching for immortal souls, dragging them down to their abysm; and every time they clutch with skeleton fingers, hearts are breaking, and homes are falling, and desolations are accumulating. Do you know there are men who do nothing else but try to draw souls into this whirlpool?

The first time I ever saw the city—it was the city of Philadelphia—I was a mere lad. I stopped at a hotel, and I remember in the even-tide one of these men plied me with his infernal art. He saw I was green. He wanted to show me the sights of the town. He painted the path of sin until it looked like emerald; but I was afraid of him. I shoved back from the basilisk—I made up my mind he was a basilisk. I remember how he wheeled his chair round in front of me, and, with a concentred and diabolical effort, attempted to destroy my soul; but there were good angels in the air that night. It was no good resolution on my part, but it was the all-encompassing grace of a good

God that delivered me. Beware! beware! oh, young man. "There is a way that seemeth right unto a man, but the end thereof is death."

If all the victims of this temptation, in all lands and ages, could be gathered together, they would make a host vaster than that which Xerxes led across the Hellespont, than that which Napoleon marshaled at Austerlitz, than that which Wellington led into Waterloo; and if they could be stretched out in single file across this continent, I think the van-guard of the host would stand on the beach of the Pacific, while yet the rear-guard stood on the beach of the Atlantic.

But I must close the black lids of this fearful subject. It seems as if for the last hour I have been walking through a leprous lazaretto. Groans on every side, and the air heavy with moral contagion. I am preaching this sermon, not because I expect to reclaim any one that has gone astray in this fearful path, but because I want to utter a warning for those who still maintain their integrity. The cases of reclamation are so few, probably you do not know one of them. I have seen a

good many start out on that road. How
many have I seen come back? Not one that
I now think of. It seems as if the spell of
death is on them, and no human voice nor the
voice of God can break the spell. Their feet
are hoppled. Their wrists are handcuffed.
They have around them a girdle of reptiles,
bunched at the waist, fastening them to an
iron doom; and every time they breathe, the
forked tongues strike them, and they strain to
break away, until the tendons snap and the
blood exudes; and in the contortions of the
eternally destroyed they cry out, "Take me
back to my father's house! Where is mother? Take me home! Take me home!"

But no, I do not believe there is one out of
five thousand that ever comes back. It seems
as if the infatuation is fatal. One went forth
from a bright Christian home. There was no
reason why she should forsake it; but induced
by unclean novelette literature and by theatre-going, she started off, and sat down at
the banquet of devils. Every few weeks she
would come back to her father's house, and
hang up her hat and shawl in the old place,

as though she expected to stay; but in a few hours, as though hounded by an inexorable fate, she would take down again the hat and the shawl, and start out. When they called her back she slammed the door in their faces, and cried, "Oh, mother! it's too late!"

Do I stand before a man to-day, the locks of whose strength are being toyed with? Let me tell you to escape, lest the shears of destruction take your moral and your spiritual integrity. Do you not see your sandals beginning to curl on that red-hot path? This day, in the name of Almighty God, I tear off the beautifying veil and the embroidered mantle of this old hag of iniquity, and I show you the ulcers, and the bloody ichor, and the cancered lip, and the eaten-up nostril, and the parting joints, and the macerated limbs, and the wriggling putrefaction, and I cry out, "Oh, horror of horrors!"

May the lightnings of an incensed God strike every house of shame, and consume all the tons of an impure literature, and write on the heavens, in capitals of fire a mile high, "All whoremongers and adulterers and sorcerers shall have their place in the lake that burneth with fire and brimstone, which is the second death."

May God forbid that any of you who have been invited into the ways of pleasantness and the paths of peace should turn your back on your safety and happiness, and go to sit down in a dungeon, where the eternally destroyed forever grind in the mills of despair, their locks shorn, and their eyes out. Samson ungianted.

THE END.

TALMAGE'S SERMONS.

SERMONS BY T. DE WITT TALMAGE, DELIVERED IN THE BROOKLYN TABERNACLE.

First Series.

12mo, *Cloth* - - - - - - - - - - - - - - - - - - - $2 00

Second Series.

12mo, *Cloth* - - - - - - - - - - - - - - - - - - $2 00

Third Series.

"*Old Wells Dug Out.*" 12mo, *Cloth* - - - - - $2 00

Fourth Series.

"*Sports that Kill.*" 12mo, *Cloth*, $1 25 ; *Paper*, $1 00

The Sermons of T. De Witt Talmage have received much attention from the press and the public. Below are given a few of the notices:

A San Francisco (California) paper, speaking of Mr. Talmage's sermons in that city, says : "We believe that no such Christian preaching has been heard since the days when George Whitefield and the two Wesleys preached the Gospel on the shores of America. Sublime in his powers of pathetic and lucid description, terrible in the earnestness with which he pleads the cause of the undying soul, overwhelming with the tender overtures of redeeming mercy, and sparkling with graceful images and illustrative anecdote, the great multitude becomes as one man beneath his touch, and a silence broken only by an occasional gasping for breath from the whole assembly, attends his utterances from the first sentence to the last."

They are the keenest, sharpest, and most vigorous specimens of pulpit oratory we have yet read.—*St. Johns* (N. B.) *Globe.*

We believe that for originality, power, and splendor, these sermons will bear comparison with the greatest pulpit productions of any age or country. But for the knowledge of human life, and the adaptation of divine truth to the whole being of man—intellectual, emotional, moral, practical — and for the power of applying that truth, we know not his equal.—*Christian Age*, London.

These sermons I regard as among the best specimens of the simple, earnest, and pungent presentation of the solemn and precious truths of the Gospel that I have ever read, and having a fertility of illustration that is marvelous. I feel earnestly desirous that they should be in a form to preach to ministers of the Gospel, and so help them to preach to others.—Rev. E. D. G. PRIME, D.D., *New York Observer*.

Mr. Talmage is clear out of the old grooves and ruts of pulpit effort. You can not measure him by the books or criticise him by the schools. He is a law unto himself. In short, he is a mystery, a phenomenon, a contradiction of all the rules and books, and a most potent power for good. He speaks to more living people in this country than any other man; and his sermons being published both in this country and in England, his influence is wider felt than that of any other Protestant minister in the world.—*Central Christian Advocate*.

The *New York Independent* says: "The new Tabernacle is massive. It will hold nearly twice as many people as Plymouth Church. Mr. Talmage is a pulpit phenomenon. His conceptions of men and things are so vivid that he can not be said to possess them — they possess him. He is dramatic, and can not describe without acting. He has a clear, incisive mind, a broad and genial humor, a high and exacting conscientiousness, kindly sympathy, a vivid imagination, vehement passion, and every blow tells."

We found ourselves in Dr. Talmage's immense audience-room containing seats for 5000 persons, with decorated ceiling, brilliant chandeliers, and spacious galleries. When the exercises began, not a foot of sitting or standing room was anywhere visible. The whole scene of the evening proved that it does not require an intermingling of heresy to fill churches. Here were crowds flocking to hear the most plain and pungent preaching on the old theme of Gospel salvation.—*Advance*, Chicago, Ill.

Mr. SPURGEON, of London, says: "Mr. Talmage's discourses lay hold of my inmost soul. The Lord is with this mighty man of valor. So may he ever be till the campaign closes with victory! I am indeed glad of his voice. It cheers me intensely. He loves the Gospel, and believes in *something*, which some preachers hardly do. There are those about who use the old labels, but the articles are not the same. May the Lord win armies of souls to Jesus by this man! I am astonished when God blesses *me*, but somehow I should not be so much surprised if he blessed this man."

Mr. Talmage's sermons have ten readers in Great Britain where any other American sermons have one reader.—D. L. MOODY.

There is about Talmage a vehemence, an urgency, an earnestness, which sometimes carries him away as in a kind of wild whirlwind. He has immense command of words, and great fluency of speech. But he is not diffuse—any thing but that. His sentences, some of them especially, fall with a force and a strength which is sometimes almost painful. There is a reckless *abandon* about many of his sermons, a hearty outspokenness, which is as refreshing as a dip into a mountain stream on a hot summer's day. He has now the largest congregation and perhaps the most powerful church in America.—*Northern Echo*, Hartlepool, England.

With an earnestness of appeal and a power of awakening that we have never heard surpassed, Dr. Talmage preaches the Old Gospel that kindled the enthusiasm of the rustic and unlettered apostles of Galilee, and at the same time elicited the zeal and influenced the heart of the cultured Pharisee of Tarsus.—*London Christian World*.

Mr. Talmage's sermons are thoroughly evangelical, and are receiving the widest attention. He is the most popular preacher of the day.—*The Methodist*.

There is a tremendous nervous energy in Mr. Talmage's sentences. They startle by their very boldness. He does not know how to soften a denunciation, or kid-glove a lie, cheat, or sham.—*Providence* (R. I.) *Press*.

Glowing with impassioned fervor, Mr. Talmage wages a deadly war against the vices of the day in their most enticing forms.—*New York Tribune*.

Dr. Talmage went to and fro with quiet step on that large platform, sinking his voice, now full of melody, almost to a whisper, yet ever audible, now rising up into an impassioned burst of unmistakable eloquence, exceeding any thing we have ever heard since the early days of Father Gavazzi. When he had ended, it seemed like the ceasing of exquisite music. For two or three minutes there was a profound silence, until the congregation seemed to arouse themselves from the thrall. Then the vast multitude dispersed.—*Liverpool* (Eng.) *Weekly Mercury.*

In many respects Mr. Talmage stands at the head of American pulpit orators, and none excel him in dramatic force.—*St. Louis Times.*

We have known persons to drop the novel half finished, and take up Talmage's sermons, never to exchange truth for trash again.—*Pittsburg Methodist Recorder.*

They are brimful of vitality, intense dramatic power of description, and an earnestness of conviction in what is said that impresses the reader deeply.—*New Orleans Picayune.*

A Baptist pastor in Michigan says: "Within a distance of ten miles there are five places (some of them school-houses) where every Sabbath people come together to hear Dr. Talmage's sermons read. They have been blessed in many conversions."

Talmage is in some respects superior to any living preacher. His book is as readable as a romance, and a world more profitable.—*Ladies' Repository*, Cincinnati.

Do we consider the great influence of a popular preacher of the present day? Neither Jeremy Taylor, Smith, or even Whitefield, had the opportunities given to Mr. Talmage through the press.—*Union Advocate.*

That Mr. Talmage is a popular preacher can not be denied, as he addresses the largest audience in Brooklyn, and perhaps the largest regular audience in America. He fulfills Garrick's idea of a preacher, and talks of religion as if it were really a matter of supreme importance. His sermons read like plays, and must entertain, if they do not convert, his hearers; but we have no reason to doubt the latter, and commend them to such as enjoy this class of literature.—*Commercial*, Cincinnati.

What building would be big enough to hold the congregation if such sermons were preached in London?—*Congregationalist*, London.

The sermons by this celebrated divine are among the most admirable compositions in the language.—*Springfield Advertiser*.

Mr. Talmage's descriptive powers are unique and of a high order; in fact, we do not know of any preacher like him.—*Pittsburg Times*.

In the author's happiest style, and outside of its religious merits, which are of a high order, it is more interesting than a romance. Nothing but the breaking down of the press can prevent this book having an immense sale.—*Reading Times*.

Mr. Talmage is a finished speaker, with a terse and nervous style. —*Irish Citizen*.

Dr. Talmage's sermons are more interesting, simply as literary works, than many novels.—*Keystone*, Philadelphia.

Through this book Mr. Talmage will preach to nearly all the world. —*Turf, Field, and Farm*.

Their power for good can scarcely be overestimated. Whether heard or read, they produce a powerful impression, and are of the kind best adapted to reach the masses in these days of absorbing worldliness and eager pursuit of gain.—*Christian Advocate*.

Mr. Talmage has proved that he can gather a regular Sabbath congregation of five thousand hearers, and that he can make himself effectively heard by that number of people. He is one of those preachers who really belong to mankind at large. Most people who try to describe Dr. Talmage begin by saying that he is like somebody, or unlike somebody else. Now the fact is that he is not like any other person at all: he is just "Talmage" all over, with as much marked individuality as ever was concentrated in any one man.—*Union Era*.

Dr. Talmage is a star of commanding lustre in the pulpit of the North. His living thoughts and burning words, on the wings of the lightning and by the agency of the press, are borne to millions who have never heard his voice nor seen his face.—*Daily Sun*, Atlanta, Ga.

Not a single page of his books can be designated as superfluous or tiresome.—*St. Louis Republican*.

We doubt not that Dr. Talmage has gained greater celebrity than any man of his age.—*Christian Advocate*, Raleigh, N. C.

Mr. Talmage preaches twice every Sunday to immense audiences. Every seat up to the rafters is filled. His manner is so impassioned, his style so original, and his figures so vivid and startling, that he holds his hearers spell-bound to the end, and he moves them to tears or smiles at will.—*Charleston News and Courier.*

We thought last evening, as we looked over Mr. Talmage's audience, now hushed so that we could hear the clock's solemn ticking keeping time to the speaker's utterances—people seemingly afraid to breathe, lest they might lose a word—we thought to ourselves, here is the perfection of oratory; here is dominion, absolute and undisputed. The attempt to do any thing but listen to those sentences—now short, sharp, and ringing, and now drawn out with a plaintiveness that will linger after his voice has died away—is so vain that it needs only to be mentioned and tried to show his power.—*Free Press*, Easton, Pa.

Almost exactly such criticisms as are brought against him were brought against Luther, and against Whitefield and Wesley. But as in them all, so in Mr. Talmage, there are elements of power that the critics of words and phrases can not comprehend. Mr. Talmage is a genuine pulpit orator; and his oratory is none the less effective because it does not conform to pulpit canons. He wins his battles, as did Napoleon, by his violation of all rules. These sermons give a hint of the moral power that lies behind Mr. Talmage's burning eloquence and gives it force.—*Christian Weekly.*

In Dr. Talmage's sermons there are portions of writing which, for thrilling interest, are not surpassed by the pages of fiction.—*The Age*, Philadelphia.

There is apparently no hidden spring in the human heart that Dr. Talmage does not know how to reach.—*Occident*, San Francisco, Cal.

Mr. Talmage has two continents for a congregation. In addition to the host that greet him every Sabbath, the *Methodist* prints one of his sermons every week; the *Interior*, of Chicago, gives his "Friday Evening Addresses;" the *Christian Age*, of London, gets the advanced sheets of his sermons (phonographically reported) for weekly publication; and other foreign papers are publishing his sermons and addresses. His discourses have appeared in book form in London, and are securing wide transatlantic attention.—*Brooklyn Eagle.*

If ministers would more generally break away from the staid niceties and etiquetical mannerism of religious service, and cry aloud, using every opportunity and every available means to arrest the attention of the people, all the while, like Talmage, preaching the primitive Gospel of Jesus—telling the "old, old story," it would be far better for the Church in all its branches.—*Pittsburg Recorder.*

The sermons published in this series speak for themselves. They are printed exactly in the words delivered, and were all extempore. What precision, memory, directness, genius, and originality they reveal need not be stated. They are more condensed than theorems, as rounded, pointed, and polished as essays, yet extemporaneous, and their preservation dependent upon reporters' pencils. Considering that Mr. Talmage is still a comparatively young man, he has won a celebrity as a preacher of which the church represented by him with such intense, earnest, and fervent eloquence may well be proud.—*Chicago Inter-Ocean.*

Mr. Talmage is one of the most pathetic and eloquent men of the age. His published works are models of Anglo-Saxon style.—*Methodist Recorder.*

He is a fearless antagonist to all forms of sin—a writer who cares more for cleaving a helmet than for showing the jewels on the handle of his weapon. Blows are what he gives; and yet, as the blade goes swiftly down, the jewels frequently flash on the eye. The raciness and abandonment to his work, conspicuous in all the writer says, will find eager readers everywhere.—*Interior.*

These sermons certainly unveil to us the secret of Mr. Talmage's extraordinary power as a preacher. * * * The great themes of experimental piety and holy living are sent home upon the hearts of men with remarkable directness, force, and fervor. Mr. Talmage has a strong imagination, which seldom flags in word-painting, and usually arrays the most common truths in all the freshness of new discoveries, and all the glow of living reality. To this he adds a quick insight into human nature, the foibles, vices, and iniquities of the day, and the Gospel as the only remedy for human corruption. All is swayed by an overmastering Christian earnestness.—*Presbyterian Quarterly.*

Mr. Talmage's knowledge of human nature, his sparkling humor, his pruning-hook as well as his scalping-knife, his deep and clear comprehension of what is spiritually beautiful, as well as his hatred of all that is radically wrong, together with his own pure Christian life and experience—all conspire to make his utterances and practical work a blessing to those who hear or read his discourses.—*Industrial Monthly*.

A writer from South Australia says: "I read every Sabbath the choice and soul-stirring sermons of Dr. Talmage to the people. Every one is delighted to hear them."

They are the product of strong thought, a red-hot heart, a tremendous earnestness, and a determined purpose to do something for Jesus Christ. So he says many things that other men omit to say, and passes by many things that they do say. The book is a live one, and we welcome it.—*Northern Christian Advocate*.

Besides performing all the functions of a minister and pastor, Mr. Talmage conducts his "Lay College," and writes from four to five columns a week for his *Christian at Work*. Within five years he has built two immense and costly churches—the second replacing the first, which was destroyed by fire. Mr. Talmage works steadily on at the same high pressure, without giving the slightest evidence of fatigue.—*Zion's Herald*, Boston.

Published by HARPER & BROTHERS, New York.

☞ Harper & Brothers *will send the above works by mail, postage prepaid, to any part of the United States, on receipt of the price.*

www.ingramcontent.com/pod-product-compliance
Lightning Source LLC
Chambersburg PA
CBHW020406230426
43664CB00009B/1201